ALIEN
Scene-by-Scene

ALIEN
Scene-by-Scene

John David Ebert

© 2015 John David Ebert
All rights reserved

ISBN: 978-1-5172142-4-1

Acknowledgements

Special thanks go to Lawrence Pearce and Tom Ebert.

Cover artwork:
"The Pelagic Argosy Sights Land" by Lawrence Pearce (2015)

Contents

Introduction to the Metaphysical Vulva   11

Opening Title Sequence   23

Awakening   29

The Crew   33

Not-Earth   39

The Landing   45

Excursion   51

Space Jockey   57

Eggs   63

Face-Hugger   67

Confrontations   75

Chest Burster   81

Epidermis   87

Labyrinth   95

Ash   103

Parker and Lambert   113

Underworld	119
Auto-Destruct	123
Final Battle	127
Appendix I:	
On the Sign Regimes in *Alien*	133
Appendix 2:	
Comparative Table of World Ages	137
Endnotes	143
Bibliography	151

Introduction to the Metaphysical Vulva

In Ridley Scott's 1979 classic film *Alien,* the central struggle—as I argue throughout this book—is that regarding the right to possess what I am going to term "the metaphysical vulva." This idea is a sort of counterweight to the Lacanian phallus, for the vulva simply does not have a place in the system of Lacan. There are specific reasons for this, since—as Derrida rightly pointed out—Lacan makes the phallus a privileged signifier within his system, and according to Derrida, a privileged signifier is the mark of a continuation of the logocentric age. Derrida therefore designates Lacan's thinking as "phallogocentric," which indeed, it is.[1]

According to Lacan, the phallus exists within his three registers of the real, the imaginary and the symbolic. The real phallus is the biological organ of the penis itself and requires no further elaboration. The imaginary phallus, however, forms part of the Pre-Oedipal triad between mother and child, and exists only in the child's mind as a fantasy image. Mother is always "elsewhere" and in order to account for her absences, the child theorizes that she is interested in the Other phallus. The child, therefore, tries to *be* the phallus for the mother in order to gain her full attention, but successful castration only occurs with the intervention of a fourth term in the triad (i.e. the father) who has the "real phallus" that forces the child to realize that it cannot *be* the phallus for the mother and so must give up trying. Desire for the mother must therefore accede to the Name of the Father, in which authority is transferred from the sphere of the mother to that of the symbolic order which the father represents. Lacan regards the father as *the* supremely spiritual figure.[2] Castration thus becomes successful only when the child defers to the paternal authority.

The symbolic phallus, however, becomes for Lacan the primary signifier in the differentiation of the full grown adult sexes, for it signifies "the desire for the Other." It is the master signifier of the relations between the sexes and governs their *jouissance*. Though the man has the real phallus, the woman's psyche comes equipped with a semiotic vacancy in which the symbolic phallus is present by its very absence. In other words, she does not have it and so always wants it in some form or another—scattered like the pieces of the dead body of Osiris as various glittering *objets petit a*—while the male has it only on the condition that his castration has been successful during childhood. But a privileged signifier like the symbolic phallus marks it as a holdover from the metaphysical age, which is synonymous (more or less) with Derrida's "logocentrism." Suffice it to say that the vulva simply does not exist in Lacan's thinking.

Lacan was operating under the shadow of Freud's patriarchal system of thought and, as is well known, Freud's patriarchy against Jung's matriarchy was the real, deep cause of their split in 1912. Jung had read his Bachofen and knew the history of mythology in much greater detail than Freud, and he was well aware of the existence of a matriarchal-matrilineal epoch that existed *before* the patriarchy of the metaphysical age (the Swiss philosopher Jean Gebser designates the equivalent of that age as the "mental consciousness structure").³

In attempting to unlock the semiotics of *Alien*, however, I don't think there is any way to truly understand the film without positing a "metaphysical vulva" as a signifier over against Lacan's phallus. The metaphysical vulva could also be said to have three registers, for it, too, exists on the real, the imaginary and the symbolic levels. And contrary to Lacan's insistences, it too has been a *very* coveted object throughout history.

The real vulva is simply this or that specific and particular vagina, just like Lacan's real phallus corresponding to the biological organ of the penis. The *imaginary* vulva, however, was an image that was privileged during the pre-metaphysical age (which Gebser designates as the age of the mythical consciousness structure) in which it is found as a mythological image all over the world. The so-called Celtic *Sheela na gig*, for instance, (shown above) in which a mythological female stretches back both labia of her vulva with two hands would be merely one example. The carved vaginas scraped onto the walls of Paleolithic caves, or carefully incised into the artwork of the famous Venus figurines of the same era, would be another.

The key thing about the imaginary vulva in its early pre-metaphysical incarnations is that it has the power to give birth spontaneously: that is to say that it does not require insemination by a male. It is analogous to the power of the earth which spontaneously brings forth its vegetation (although both ancient and contemporary men knew very well that seeds were required for this act of creative spontaneity. However, in the psyche, the earth producing its own vegetation is an image that is a little like the rising of the sun: we know, in post-Copernican times, that the sun does not rise at all but that it is the effect of the earth's rotation on its axis. But we still continue to say, and to feel at dawn as we watch the rosy-fingers creep their way across the lavender sky, that it does indeed "rise" no matter what science says about it).

The myth of the *spartoi* (i.e. "sown men") is a classic example of the power of the imaginary vulva. When Cadmus, the bringer of the alphabet from Phoenicia to Greece, was told by the Delphic oracle to follow a certain cow and to found a city wherever it stopped, he came to the area of Thebes and prepared to sacrifice it. In order to sacrifice the cow, however, he required water, so he sent his men to fetch some, but the nearby spring was guarded by a dragon sacred to Ares. Cadmus slew the dragon for them and was then told by Athena to sow its teeth into the earth, and when he did so, armed men sprang from furrows out of the ground as a race of warriors. Cadmus, fearing their might, threw a stone—or some versions say a jewel—into the midst of them, over which they fought until only five warriors emerged and it was these five warriors that helped

Cadmus build the city of Thebes.

This is thus a type of myth in which the power of the earth to bring forth life from the metaphysical vulva—on its imaginary register—is demonstrated. The myth of Deucalion is a similar example, in which the flood survivor is told to repopulate the human race by casting the bones of his mother over his shoulder. The bones are rocks thrown over his shoulder, and they metamorphose, by the power of Gaia herself, into human beings. In Indian mythology, likewise, Sita (whose name means "furrow"), the famous consort of Rama who is kidnapped by the demon Ravana in *The Ramayana*, was said to have been simply born from the fields while her father King Janaka was ploughing them.

On the first pages of Hesiod's *Theogony*, likewise, the power of the imaginary vulva is demonstrated in the parthenogenetic myth of Chaos spontaneously giving birth to the goddess Gaia, who then in turn gives birth to Eros and Tartaros.[4] These are births that do not require insemination by a male, and they are vestigial survivals into later myth of very, very old ideas about the Mother Goddess, analogously to Mother Earth, spontaneously producing offspring. (The latest and most recent descendant of this myth occurs in David Cronenberg's 1979 film *The Brood*, in which Frank Carveth's wife Nola is taught by an experimental psychiatrist how to externalize her rage in the form of physical flesh by simply brooding a gang of angry children from a uterine sac that grows externally to her actual biological womb. She proudly tears one of these sacs open with her teeth in order to show her horrified husband that she has retrieved the ancient parthenogenetic ability of the goddess to give birth without sexual intercourse [*parthenos* means "virgin"]. His disgust, however, enrages her and so the children, who are physicalized extensions of her anger, come after him).

The metaphysical vulva on the *symbolic plane*, however, is a structural feature of the metaphysical age proper that begins with the Greeks and the Jews, whose myths are filled with male deities performing their own acts of parthenogenesis that they have stolen from the goddesses and earth mothers of the preceding mythical age. Zeus, for instance, gives birth to Dionysus in this way, for when he impregnated Semele and she demanded to see him in his true form, she was burnt to cinders by his lightning-like apotheosis. Zeus managed to preserve the fetus of Dionysus, however, which survived the blast, by having it sewn into his thigh, from whence he gave birth to the god. This is a type of myth that marks the appropriation of the imaginary vulva from the goddess (where it has now attained a *symbolic* status), at the onset of the metaphysical age (which Jean Gebser in *his* terminology designates the mental consciousness structure. See Appendix 2 for a comparative table of world ages).[5]

During the metaphysical age, then, the vulva is taken over by the patriarchal gods introduced by the Indo-Aryans into the various civilizations of Greece, the Middle East and India during the entire second millennium before Christ. Even in India, where the goddess later took *back* her imaginal vulva, (the lotus which is, in that tradition, symbolic of the vulva), and upon which goddesses once sat, was appropriated by a male god named Brahma, and the lotus reassigned by a sort of umbilical cord to the dreaming god Vishnu. Brahma usurped the creative powers of the goddess Maya by emanating Vishnu's dream out into the four directions with his four faces to become the world of waking daylight consciousness. (This masculine usurpation didn't last long in India, though, which is the one place on the planet where the age old goddess, going back to Harappan times [circa 2500 BC], reasserted her lotus power in various forms, such as that of Durga, the monster slayer created by the male gods who were unable themselves to slay the buffalo demon that was ravaging the land).

In the Hebrew world, however, God created Eve by pulling a rib forth from the side of Adam. Men were now imagined as having the creative ability to give birth to women. Later, Yahweh would make use of the pristine uterus of Mary by proxy in order to breathe forth the creative Logos, as the Word made flesh, into the world of physical matter as an Evental (i.e. *Ereignis*) singularity.

The myths of the early half of the metaphysical age laid down the foundations for the separation of Being from Becoming when it came time for the development of that high intellectual mode of discourse which we know as "philosophy." According to Heidegger, during the time of the Pre-Socratics, Being was understood as *physis*, a mode of entities arising and self-manifesting their essences as numinous beings. By the time of Plato, however, Being became divorced from the flow of time and Becoming—flows of time are traditionally symbolized by rivers, which in turn are often associated with goddesses, especially in India—and was now understood in the mode of *eidos*, in which the transcendental Forms and Ideas existed in their own realm separate from the flow of physical entities and which it was the job of the true philosopher to master.[6] Poets, those children of the Muses, were accordingly banished from Plato's ideal academy and the metaphysical age—as Heidegger designated it—was by then in full operation.

The symbolic vulva is thus a *deterritorialized* vulva. It is the vulva as it existed during the metaphysical age from the time of about 1200 BC down to the age of Heidegger and Modernism (although it still survives, vestigially, in the metaphysical matrices of Big Science corporations). Deleuze and Guattari, in their 1980 book *A Thousand Plateaus*, fleshed out this concept of deterritorialization by giving a few concrete examples: the human hand, for instance, is a deterritorialized animal paw.[7] The human mouth, an organ with curved lips originally designed for sucking nourishment out of nipples, was deterritorialized from the function of nourishment and then *re*-territorialized for the function of language, which Heidegger famously termed in his essay, "Letter on Humanism," as the "house of Being," which is kept carefully clean and swept in zen monk fashion by poets, who are its guardians and architects.[8] (Note that Heidegger's attitude toward poets, at the end of the metaphysical age [which he calls a time of the "darkening of Being,"] as it is shifting into the *post*-metaphysical age, is diametrically opposed to Plato's).[9]

During the metaphysical age—which lasted for about three thousand years—the metaphysical vulva was deterritorialized from its imaginary order in the imagery of female-dominant myths and then *re*-territorialized as a symbolic signifier possessed by world-shaping demiurges and male creator deities who used it to perform the function of generativity, but generativity by the power of the spoken (and later, written) Word, rather than by biological forces. Notice that the creative power shifted from the zone of the genitals to that of the head, inside which the vulva became interiorized as a symbolic orifice giving birth to Ideas.

The vitality of the word—especially as mediated by the Greco-Semitic invention and proliferation of the alphabet— became the West's most powerful metaphysical instrument. The sung word, for instance, became the basis for Gregorian chant, from out of which classical music was born, and the variously translated texts of Aristotle, at about the same time, became the basis for the creation of the Medieval university in Paris and London. Indeed, God's creative power became so identified with that of the word that by the time Descartes utters the phrase, "I think, therefore I am," the power of Being to assert its factual existence is still based upon the power of thought—*trained* thought, disciplined by reading books—to form Ideas.

The eventual rise of the Machine Age during the Industrial Revolution that then followed during the late eighteenth century had the ultimate outcome, as Heidegger put it, of "enframing" and surrounding the earth with technical systems.[10] Today, the planet is not adorned with occasional machines; rather, it actually exists *inside* of a gigantic machine of global scale that has swallowed it up entire, like Saturn devouring his children. The metaphysical vulva, in the making of this global apparatus, was deterritorialized from the earth itself—as well as the human body--and completely appropriated by science in order to rival its creative powers.

Make no mistake about it: science—especially that embodied by Big Science institutions in the form of corporations like Monsanto or Genentech—now *owns* and patents the metaphysical vulva. The power to create new life through genetic engineering in the form of pest-resistant crops, or in vitro fertilization, (or in the case of the sheep named Dolly, actual replication through cloning), is now the *exclusive* prerogative of a science that has been bequeathed to us from the myths of the metaphysical age which began with the vulva being taken from the imaginary order and translated to the status of a signifier in the symbolic order of language and the power of the Word to actually create, and make, material forms.

In Ridley Scott's *Alien*, then, this power—that of the metaphysical vulva—is precisely what is at issue as a new race of Furies in the form of H.R. Giger's alien creatures is inadvertently unleashed from their confinement in the underworld and let loose into the interior of a spacecraft that functions as a miniature world island designed by Father Science to replicate the life-sustaining environmental conditions of Gaia (i.e. sleep, food, artificial gravity, oxygen and other life-fostering functions).

The alien in Scott's film, as I will argue throughout this book, is part of an *Other* regime, not the sign regime of the metaphysical age that gave rise to Lacan's paternal metaphor and his phallogocentrism, but the retrieval of an *older* regime that the metaphysical age displaced by banishing all its signifiers, during the course of various wars against *nagas* and Titans, to the (Western) underworld.

It is the alien in this film which has all the self-organizing creative power, not the crew of the engineering marvel of the spaceship *Nostromo*. It is the alien who outsmarts them all with its astonishing and rapidly cycling metamorphoses which are always a step ahead of them. It is the alien which swallows up and engulfs this miniature world island constructed by Father Science. It is the alien which claims the *right* to create biomorphic forms through the power of parthenogenetic self-organization. And it is the crew who loses out.

But, unlike *Moby Dick*, in which Melville's famous whale destroys the *Pequod* and kills everyone except Ishmael, the creature in *Alien* is finally killed in the end. It is, after all, a monster slayer myth created by an ever-optimistic Hollywood whose executives with their phallogocentrism could never allow the monster to win *completely* (although that was precisely Ridley Scott's original plan going into the production).

The alien *is* killed.

But by a woman.

And therein lies the rub, as the following pages will uncover.

Opening Title Sequence
(0:00 – 2:41)

The film opens on a shot of outer space, while the camera slowly pans from left to right across a dusky planet with vanilla-colored rings surrounding it. Left to right, it should be remembered, is the direction in which Westerners read lines of text (the direction preferred by the Greeks), a cultural custom that is considered by the Swiss philosopher Jean Gebser as an orientation that moves *from* the unconscious toward further expanding and awakening of consciousness to the outer world.[11] That very increase in the awakening of consciousness eventually led the West to master the laws of perspectival space and to see and visualize space as an empty container inside which objects, things, or entities were all scaled to the same dimensions. This gave the West its ability to create the kinds of complex machines—visualized as objects in three-dimensional space--that have led to the construction of mega-mechanical monstrosities such as the spaceship that we are about to see enter the frame in a moment.

Meanwhile, as the camera pans from left to right, the film's title begins to piece itself together, beginning with the letter "I" at the top (middle) of the screen, unfolding as a series of obscure vertical lines. Notice that the letters do not form themselves in a left to right reading sequence, but seem to spontaneously self-organize from the center outwards (the title, in other words, is already a compressed version of the alien's strategy of exploding from within outwards). At one point, there are five vertical slashes which Ridley Scott specifically thought should evoke some kind of strange hieroglyphic language (a language that, because it does not read from left to right, would be "alien" to Western sensibilities). Thus, there is already an "otherness" built into the film's title sequence. Once the opposite half of the vertical slash of the letter "A" has formed, however, the viewer then knows that it is going to spell out "Alien," the film's title, and the otherness begins to recede back into the familiar.

Note that alien hieroglyphics are never encountered in the film, however. When the crew of the *Nostromo* discover the derelict spacecraft on the dusty planetoid, they find alien beings—one dead alien and many living eggs—but no hieroglyphics are ever found.[12] Scott's title sequence alludes to a discarded idea that was part of the film's original screenplay, in which the crew was supposed to find the alien derelict first, and *then* shortly afterwards, discover a pyramid or "egg-silo" (where the alien eggs were to be kept) in which one of the crew—probably Kane—was to be let down through the top of the pyramid and would find inscribed on its walls an alien hieroglyphic script. The scene was dropped because it was considered to be both costly as well as potentially slowing the film down, but it was revived and reused for Ridley Scott's 2012 prequel to the film, *Prometheus*, which features a title sequence that similarly pieces itself together like the original title sequence of *Alien*. Also, the crew of the spaceship *Prometheus* discover, not a derelict spacecraft, but precisely the kind of temple or pyramid inside which an alien language is written in a hieroglyphic script that only the android David—because he has been studying all the world's languages--is able to read.

Also, the letters of *Alien* that piece themselves together suggest something autonomous that self-organizes, like an alien life form. The letters have their own autonomy and obey their own (non-Western) program. They are, as I have remarked, a compressed and miniaturized illustration of the process of morphogenesis whereby forms spontaneously bring themselves into being through self-organization from noise.

Once the credits have finished, the camera then pans to a shot of the depths of outer space where a dark and shadowy spacecraft is simply drifting along like a ghost ship (already alluding to its eventual fate). There are no lights on it, and it seems to float without direction, as though adrift on some invisible cosmic ocean. (In reality, it is "asleep," for its crew are all in cryo-sleep, but it is about to be "awakened," once again illustrating Gebser's principle of the awakening of consciousness).

A legend then appears which informs us that the ship is the *Nostromo*—named after Joseph Conrad's novel of the same title (the ship, in early drafts of the screenplay, was originally called the *Leviathan)* since Ridley Scott had been reading quite a bit of Conrad at the time—and the legend also says that the ship is carrying a crew of seven. It is so large because it has a built-in refinery and a cargo of 20,000,000 tons of mineral ore that the crew has been busy mining from other planets. The last line of the legend tells us that the ship's present course is headed back home for earth.

That there are precisely *seven* crewmembers is interesting in light of the fact that in the cosmology of the ancients, there were also seven heavenly bodies: sun, moon, Mars,

Mercury, Jupiter, Venus and Saturn. This heavenly hierarchy then became the basis of our seven-day week, each day standing for one of the seven celestial spheres.

Alan Dean Foster's novelization of the film says that the rig is specifically hauling petroleum and that its refinery is busy processing that into fuel, but Scott's legend only specifies "mineral ore." The basis of alchemy rested on an earlier, and much older—possibly Babylonian—theory that minerals and precious metals like tin and copper are analogized to embryos located inside of their ore, embryos that, given time, would naturally ripen into the more noble metals.[13] Metallurgy is thus thought of as the process of human intervention to shorten the life cycle of the mineral to bring it to its more "perfect" form. So already, there is a subtle reference to the embryology, as it were, of mineral ore that requires the obstetric processes of chemical treatment that will transform them into "higher" organisms. A mineralogical life-cycle, in other words.

The final shot of this opening sequence is from below the enormous spacecraft, where the camera scans along to give the viewer a sense of its massive scale. This shot is also a subtle visual quotation of both the opening scene of *Star Wars*, in which the gigantic star destroyer passes through the frame above as it engulfs Princess Leia's tiny rebel cruiser, but also the scene from *2001: A Space Odyssey*, in which Kubrick gives us the "endless" tracking shot of the scientific spaceship named the *Discovery* that is on its way, not home to earth, but rather outward bound to Jupiter.

That the *Nostromo* is headed "home" is itself an interesting detail in light of the film's many gynecological signifiers, and also—as we will see—its "matrilineal" sign regime, for the earth is the body of the mother towards which its crew of seven is headed, like the ancient myth of the soul, before birth, descending toward earth—the heaviest object in the universe in Pre-Copernican cosmology—and passing through each one of the seven celestial spheres (to become imprinted with the native qualities of each of those spheres) on its way toward incarnation into a physical body down on earth. In some of the Gnostic versions of this myth, the soul had to battle its way past the guardians of each of these spheres, guardians who were known as Archons, and which were hostile to the soul, especially on its ascent back up to its heavenly home.

The crew of the *Nostromo*, likewise, in order to get back home, will have to engage in battle with an alien species which is blocking its way and which is utterly unsympathetic to their homeward-bound nostalgia for earth.

Awakening
(2:42 – 6:42)

In the next scene, the camera exhibits the ship's empty interior, drifting down one hallway and corridor after the next. It begins on the C deck, or "garage level," which has a rounded corridor that is lined with pipes, copper tubing, wires and metal conduits of all kinds, reminding one perhaps of the inside of a submarine. The camera then moves up to B level, where it catches a glimpse of the empty mess hall, lingers for a moment near the coffee-making unit, which will soon be activated, then rounds a corner that is lined with wires, switches and buttons of various kinds in order to glimpse down another corridor leading to a central hatchway where a white ladder drops down an octagonal hole to C level, the ship's "underworld." The camera then backs away from both corridors to reveal the ship's bridge, a cramped and claustrophobic environment of seats wedged in front of low-rez video monitors, with emergency helmets perched at the tops of the seats for quick and ready access.

One of the computer consoles then bursts into life, a red view screen displaying the ship's name and identification number with parallel rows of glowing blue and red buttons beneath it. The monitors then begin to crawl with lists of data as the ship's central computer, Mother, does a quick scan that is reflected in the glass of the emergency helmets, as rows of digits file past with electronic chirping and beeping noises that go abruptly silent.

The camera then cuts to a darkened corridor that suddenly illuminates itself with a series of fluorescent tube lights that flicker on, revealing a white octagonal foyer with a closed door that is imprinted with a small red-checkered square. The door then lifts up with a hiss of air that reveals the ship's darkened cryo-chamber, where a series of seven sleeping pods radiates out from a central hub. The glass lids of the sleeping pods now raise up in tandem, as though they were the petals of some strange hydraulic flower, while the room simultaneously floods with light. The first to awaken is Kane, who rises groggily from his twelve month long sleep and blinks in the harsh white light as he climbs out of his pod. Kane reaches for the robe that he has left out beside his pod and then strides out of the cryo-chamber as the other crewmembers are beginning to stir into wakefulness behind him. (We know from earlier drafts of the screenplay, and also from Alan Dean Foster's novelization, that Kane will proceed to make coffee for everyone). But it is no coincidence that Kane is the first to awaken, since it is a foreshadowing of the fact that he will also be the first of the seven to die.

The comparison of the raising of the glass lids of the sleeping pods to the petals of a flower is not accidental, but was a deliberate intention on the part of one of the film's production designers, Les Dilley, who comments: "We really wanted the sequence, but we couldn't get it right. Then we got the idea of hydraulically operated tops that open like a flower. It worked." [14]

The sleeping pods, then, with their opening flower-like petals are a mechanical-hydraulic contrast with the later opening of the "petals" of the alien eggs—each egg has four petals—when Kane first leans in to get a closer look at one of them. The film, as we will gradually discover, has *two* sign regimes: a techno-scientific sign regime centered on and around the *Nostromo* and which functions as part for the whole—that is to say, metonymically—of the world of corporate science and engineering; and a Gigerian sign regime that is its opposed counterpart and which constitutes the biomorphic world of the aliens (which, in the film, is "alien" to the corporate scientific sensibilities of the first sign regime). The conceptual artist Ron Cobb, upon whose designs both the ship's interiors and its exterior were built, is the master craftsman of this first regime, while the Swiss artist H.R. Giger—a sort of reincarnation of Hieronymous Bosch into the twentieth century—is the creator of the film's alien "biomorphic" regime. Thus, the raising of the hydraulic lids of the cryo-pods is the first contrast between the two regimes, although this does not become evident until one reaches the later scene inside the derelict spacecraft.[15]

The other point to note about the comparison of the cryo-pods to the opening petals of a flower is that in Indian mythology the opening of the petals of a cosmic lotus refers specifically to the act of the awakening of consciousness, not only on a daily level, but also at the beginning of each of the great *yugas* and *manvantaras* of which the cosmos is subdivided temporally. Vishnu is the god who sleeps on a bed of milk-white serpents—i.e. the Milky Way—and as he dreams, a lotus rises from his naval and opens its petals. Sitting upon that lotus is the god Brahma, a god with four faces which emanate Vishnu's dream out into the four cardinal directions as the "nightmare of world history," as James Joyce calls it. Brahma is the god of waking daylight consciousness—just as Joyce's *Ulysses* is the novel that captures the banalities of humanity's daytime experiences—

while Vishnu is the god of dreaming consciousness, just as *Finnegans Wake* is the great book of humanity's nighttime existence. Shiva, then, is the god of deep dreamless sleep.

Hence, just as the *Nostromo*'s nervous system—a computer named Mother—has awakened the ship itself, so now the crew of seven space truckers has awakened on the inside of the ship as surrounding "daytime" environment. From the literal point of view, the crew of seven is inside a spaceship on its way to earth, but from the metaphoric point of view, it is the techno-scientific mind which has been awakened, the mind of industrial science which has surrounded and "enframed" the earth and is currently in process of appropriating its biomorphic powers, that is to say, its power of biological form-making.

We will see that not only is *Alien* about the conflict between two opposed sign regimes—the engineering functionality of the Cobbian world vs. the biomorphic power of the Gigerian—but that the conflict between the two regimes also involves a struggle over the power of biomorphogenesis itself. The film's semiotics revolve around the attempts of Father Science—the ultimate signifier of what Heidegger termed "the metaphysical age"[16] (and which Jean Gebser designated "the mental consciousness structure")—to appropriate the powers of the metaphysical vulva (like Lacan's phallus, it too has a real, imaginary and symbolic register, as I've posited in the Introduction). The metaphysical vulva is not the vulva that exists in the Real, which would be an actual vagina, but the imaginary and symbolic vulvas which, if Father Science can take possession of them, would confer upon him the ability to generate biological life forms artificially.

The Crew

(6:43 – 9:09)

There now follows a lap dissolve from the cryo-chamber to the mess hall, where the crew is already in the middle of eating their breakfast. The mess hall is small and cramped, with a round table illuminated by a grimy yellow pool of light. The crew sit round the table, and the camera quietly introduces us to them as it circles counterclockwise from the ship's captain Dallas, who has just glanced at his watch; Kane, to his left, has finished eating and is smoking a cigarette; and to Kane's left sit Parker and Brett, the ship's working class mechanics who are always grumbling about low wages; while to Brett's right sits Ripley, the ship's warrant officer, who is currently pouring herself another cup of coffee, while Jones, her orange cat, sits on the table beside her, lapping up his food. The camera then goes back clockwise the other way so that we may also catch Ash, the ship's science officer, who is eating a bowl of cereal while standing; and Lambert, the ship's female navigator, who is now seen sitting to Dallas's right.

Ash reaches for more milk and then sits down while Lambert complains of being cold. Parker asks his buddy Brett if he's still "with us," as he puts it, and Brett gives forth his characteristic laconic reply of "Right." Kane, in yet another foreshadowing of his fate, says that he *feels* dead. Parker then asks him if anybody's ever told him that he actually *looks* dead, which draws a few laughs from the crew.

Brett silently mouths the word "bonus" to Parker, who then insists that before they dock, they should discuss the bonus situation, to which Brett then agrees. Parker says that both he and Brett feel they are not getting equal shares in the profits, but Dallas, who has obviously heard this conversation before, tells the two mechanics that they'll get whatever they contracted for, just like everybody else. Brett points out, though, that everybody else is paid more than he and Parker.

At that moment, a buzzer goes off and Ash tells Dallas that Mother wants to speak with him, while Dallas remarks that he had already seen the yellow light indicating that whatever Mother has to say is for his eyes only.

Dallas then steps onto the cramped and half-darkened bridge in order to enter the access corridor to the ship's central computer, which is located near the mess hall. He enters a gloomy foyer, then flips a small switch to a tiny light that casts a yellow pool of incandescence on a set of buttons upon which he types his passcode that opens a catch-door, giving him the electronic key to the computer room. He inserts the key into its latch, which then flips up a small panel concealing a button which he punches, and then a series of miniature fluorescent bulbs lights up the entrance to Mother. The door slides open, while Dallas, cup of coffee still in hand, enters Mother's inner sanctum: a rounded yellow room which is covered from floor to ceiling with tiny blinking bulbs the size of Christmas tree lights and a central chair that directs the user to a small monitor in order to enable him or her to converse with the computer.

Dallas rotates the electronic chair so that it faces the central monitor, which he then brings to life by punching his keyboard and saying, "Morning, Mother." The screen, which is about the size of a small, old-fashioned television set, lights up with a glowing green geometric lattice. Dallas punches more buttons, which bring up a list of options in prehistoric green computer font, and selects the one for "Interface 2037 Ready for Inquiry." Then he types in a question: "What's the story Mother?"

In Ron Cobb's design for the *Nostromo*, he has carefully located this inner sanctum of the ship's central nervous system as the nucleus around which B level--with its mess hall, autodoc, cryo-chamber and bridge—is organized. It is therefore structurally homologous—in Sign Regime A, let's designate it—with Sign Regime B's derelict spacecraft and *its* central dome, beneath which is located a round inner chamber upon which the ship's pilot is seated (see Appendix I for a structural comparison of the two sign regimes). This would make it functionally analogous with the *Nostromo*'s bridge, from whence the ship is piloted, but morphologically homologous with Mother's round inner sanctum where the inquirer sits on a rotating chair in order to interface with her and acquire information. Mother's swarm of tiny blinking lights corresponds to the swarm of alien eggs in the derelict ship's cargo hold, which is located directly down a hatch from the space jockey's platform (which, as Scott shows us in his prequel *Prometheus*, is also designed to rotate).

Mother is, of course, a benign transformation of HAL 9000 from Kubrick's *2001: A Space Odyssey* (whereas HAL's paranoia and aggression are transferred in *Alien* to the robot Ash). Electronics, as McLuhan always used to say, constitute an *outering* of the human central nervous system,[17] and the crew inside the *Nostromo* are surrounded and protected by a uteromorphic[18]—though artificial—womb-sphere which runs the ship for them while they are asleep. They are therefore *inside* of an electronic duplicate of a mammalian womb which is entirely composed of circuits that conduct information at light speed, just as our nervous system does.

The *philosophical* idea, though, is that the *Nostromo* is a technicized replacement for the earth itself. It somehow generates artificial gravity and is constantly pumping oxygen in from canisters that are located possibly in the "underworld" of C deck, the garage level below the main deck. Speaking in terms of Theory, the ship is an example of what theoretician Peter Sloterdijk would call a "world island." Sloterdijk makes a distinction between three different types of world islands: *an absolute world island* (of which the *Nostromo* is an example) which, like a space shuttle, is implanted into a completely hostile environment that must constantly be fended off by technical and artificial means. If anything—anything at all--goes wrong with those technical means, an absolute world island can disintegrate rapidly (just as the space shuttle *Challenger*, with its frozen O rings, blew up after take off).[19] A *relative world island* would be something like Biosphere II in Oracle, Arizona, which is not situated in an environment that is totally hostile to it, but is sealed off nevertheless. If something goes wrong in a relative world island—as it did, in the case of Biosphere II—it does not necessarily mean that the island cannot be repaired and salvaged for further use. Finally, there are *anthropogenic world islands*, such as apartments located in cellular matrices inside of huge skyscrapers which are designed as incubators to support a human existence.[20]

The *Nostromo*, needless to say, is an example of an absolute world island with a fragile existence that is maintained for the crew by Mother, an artificial replacement for Gaia, the earth itself which supplies living beings with gravity, oxygen, sunlight, UV protection, etc. These things are absent on a ship in outer space, and if the slightest unwanted element intrudes into this environment, it can very quickly cause a chain reaction that will destroy the whole technical womb-sphere of the ship itself.

Hence, the danger to the crew of an immunological rupture if an unwanted biohazard is allowed through the ship's protective membrane and transforms Mother's cozy womb-sphere into one of Heiner Muhlmann's "maximal stress environments,"[21] in which bare naked existence (Agamben's *zoe*)[22] becomes a moment to moment threat.

The function of this scene for the story, however, is that it brings onstage *all* entities which are under the care and protection of their electronic Mother: seven crewmembers (six humans and one android; or, four living men and two living females); a cat; and a computer. It is Mother's job to protect them all with her exospheric world island, and if she fails in this task, the eight entities under her care (depending on how one counts them) are doomed to perish.

Not-Earth

(9:10 – 12:40)

The scene presently shifts to the bridge, where the crew is busy strapping themselves into their cramped seats. Ash and Lambert are shown getting situated, while Ripley is leaning forward muttering the word "right" (as though infected by Brett's laconic word-virus). Kane slides his seat forward and tells Lambert, sitting to his right, to plug them in, which she does, causing whole rows of luminous red and yellow lights to flash into being. Ash, from his own console, thanks her and then begins flipping switches while Lambert, the ship's navigator, sounds puzzled: "Where's earth?" she asks, rhetorically. Kane tells her that she would be the one to know, but Ripley from somewhere behind him announces that they are not even in earth's system. Kane, cigarette in hand, tells Lambert to perform a cartographical scan, and then asks Ripley to contact traffic control.

An exterior shot of the *Nostromo* then follows, while Ripley's voice, giving the *Nostromo*'s identification number, sounds through the deep deserts of outer space, sending forth a message to a base in Antarctica that receives no response. Her voice, translated into an electromagnetic pulse signal, sends forth data that will take many light years to reach the earth.

Ripley tells Kane that she is not receiving a reply and he tells her to keep trying, while Lambert then announces that she has mapped their location in a system that is just short of Zeti II Reticuli. Kane mutters, puffing on his cigarette, that *that* is hard to believe, while Lambert asks, rhetorically once more, what the hell they are doing way out here? Ripley then states, needlessly, that that's not their system, to which Lambert replies in an irritated tone of voice that she is well aware of that fact.

The scene then cuts to C deck in the narrow corridors below, where Parker and Brett are walking, while the sounds of the ship's engines can be heard surrounding them. Parker asks Brett if he ever notices how the rest of the crew never come down to C deck, and Brett replies by saying that it's for the same reason he and Parker only get half shares, "our time is their time," he says, that's just the way they see it. Parker then tells Brett that he thinks the *real* reason the rest of the crew never comes down to visit their underworld is because of Brett's lack of personality.

The scene then returns to the mess hall, where the crew have gathered round the table once again, but this time for a meeting. Parker and Brett are just arriving from C deck, and in another scene that foreshadows a future plot development, Parker tells Ash that he is sitting in Parker's customary seat (thus providing a glimpse of the confrontation between the two later, when Parker breaks off Ash's head only to discover that he is an android). Ash complies and gets up, allowing Parker to have his way (for now).

Parker then asks what's going on, while Dallas, leaning on his knee with one foot on a seat, tells them that most of the crew must have already figured out by now that they aren't anywhere near Earth, but only halfway there. Dallas then explains to them that Mother has interrupted the course of their journey because she is programmed to do so should certain conditions arise.

Ripley wants to know what conditions he's talking about, and Dallas says that it appears that Mother has intercepted a transmission of unknown origin and that they are required to check it out. Lambert asks what kind of a transmission he's talking about, and he replies that it is an acoustical beacon that repeats at intervals of every 12 seconds. Kane asks if it's an S.O.S. Dallas says he doesn't know. Ripley asks if the source is human and Dallas tells her that he doesn't know that either.

Parker then interrupts and points out that they are on a commercial vessel, not a rescue ship, but that he would be happy to participate if they were willing to pay him more money. Ash, leaning over Parker's chair (which now gives him the higher ground) cuts Parker off and tells him that there is a clause in their contract which states that any transmission that might indicate the existence of a possible intelligent life form *must* be investigated, and if it isn't, the penalty involves a total forfeiture of all shares. Parker says that he isn't interested and just wants to go home and party, but Dallas raises his voice at him and tells him to listen to what Ash is saying, who reiterates that there will be no money *at all* if they don't investigate the signal. Parker laughs it off, shrugs and says in that case, he'll be happy to play along.

In this scene, note that there are *two* distress signals, both electromagnetic in nature, that are sent forth. The first, Ripley's call to a base in Antarctica is not, technically speaking, a distress call, but rather an attempt to make contact with earth, and her message is sent beaming through infinite space in all directions. It is a message from Sign Regime A.

The story's first contact with Sign Regime B—the Gigerian alien regime—occurs in the form of an electromagnetic pulse signal, an acoustical beacon, as Dallas calls it, that might—or might not—be a distress call.

It was Marshall McLuhan who was the first to identify the structural—one might even say, architectural—components of what he termed "acoustic space" (to be contrasted with "visual space") as essentially *cavernous* in nature.[23] (Acoustic space, according to him, is also tactile; in either case, it is *non*-visual). Sound comes at us from all directions simultaneously and therefore forms what Peter Sloterdijk calls a "sonosphere" all around us.[24] Electromagnetic signals are beamed at us, likewise, from all directions and therefore retrieve the archaic sonosphere of the pre-perspectival ancients, for whom space was "cavernous" in nature, like Jean Gebser's magical consciousness structure in which the world is visualized as a sonic echo chamber, or a resonant cavern with a point-like unity in which all the earth's etheric lines interpenetrate with all the others. That is the whole basis of how magical effects can be sent, rippling across space-time, via this hidden etheric spider's web holding everything together.[25]

Visual space, on the other hand, was first fully developed during the Renaissance and is configured primarily by the eye which beholds space as a container *inside which* objects are all scaled to the same three dimensions.[26] Space is not cavernous in this configuration, but rather Infinite (think of Oswald Spengler's idea that Faustian civilization is obsessed with Infinite Space), connected and rational. It is ultimately a development out of Euclid's *Elements*, which begins with geometrical constructions based upon straight lines and right angles. As one works through Euclid's proofs, it takes a while before he starts to introduce circles, since circles are in essence "non-rational" holdovers from the pre-metaphysical age of the mythical and matrilineal consciousness structures. The whole problem of *pi*, as the radius of a circle, is that it is a non-rational number, and non-rational numbers were so mysterious to the metaphysical age mentality that the Pythagoreans outlawed them as heresies within their cult of number, logic and mystical rationality.

Thus, the acoustical beacon from Sign Regime B, which is the crew of the *Nostromo*'s first contact with any "alien" signifiers in the film, already suggests the coming discovery of the cavern-like space derelict the insides of which do not seem to follow the laws of correct perspective at all. Everything inside the derelict ship is curvilinear, non-rational, biomorphic and "alien" to the logic and right-angle-obsessed mentality of the rational consciousness structure of science.

Brett's repetition of the word "right" is precisely what the encounter of Sign Regime A with the alien Sign Regime B will *undo*. Sign Regime B will infiltrate, subvert, attack and destroy Sign Regime A, with all its masculinist attempts to control the female body and the earth's geo- and biomorphic systems themselves.

For as Derrida would point out, Sign Regime A—which, in his terminology would correspond to "the logocentric age"—is built up against Sign Regime B with certain structures that it has privileged by repressing and de-legitimizing those of Sign Regime B. Just as for Derrida, the logocentric age[27] (which is the same thing as Heidegger's metaphysical age) privileges the voice over writing, and authorial presence over its absence, and the "original" metaphysical *archai* (or "signature") over the copy, (including the collapsing of language down to single, authoritative meanings), which Derrida then proceeds to undermine through the process of deconstruction, so in *Alien*, Sign Regime A—that of the techno-scientific masculine world of Big Science—has privileged certain structures and repressed others, namely those of Sign Regime B, into a kind of "anti-spheric" underworld (which is made visible in the paintings of Hieronymous Bosch). In Sign Regime A, the male is privileged over the female; logic over the irrational; the rectilinear over the curvilinear; the artificial over the "natural"; the chemical substitute over the real thing; the absolute world island (of an artificially enclosed environment) over against the Great World Island of Mother Earth herself.

The Landing

(12:41 – 20:00)

This scene begins with the crew all gathered on the bridge in order to actually listen to the alien distress signal. Dallas asks Lambert to play the recording of the signal, while Ash seats himself nearby. A strange, ghostly metallic scraping sound then ensues as the signal plays, and Ripley comments that it doesn't sound like any signal she's ever heard. Lambert suggests that it is possibly some type of voice and Dallas says that they'll soon know as he requests her to pull up the coordinates of the planet that it is emanating from. She gives him the planetoid's declination and ascension and Dallas tells her to bring it up on the screen. Ripley leans forward to get a better view on the grainy video monitor and Lambert informs them that the orb is only 1,200 kilometers in circumference, defining it technically as a planetoid with a rotation of two hours and gravity of point eight six. Ash tells them that at least they can walk on it.

There follows an exterior shot of the *Nostromo* from below, in which its bulbous cargo holds resemble huge mechanical eggs, as the ship drifts toward the larger planet (a gas giant?) with rings around it and which is orbited by the planetoid. These industrial "eggs" with their mineral ore cargo should be contrasted with the living eggs from Sign Regime B.

Inside the ship, meanwhile, all the crew are strapped into their seats as they prepare to land on the planetoid. Ash informs them that the equatorial orbit has been found, and he watches from his console as a low-rez sketch of the ship's trajectory traces their approach to the planetoid. Ash, at least, has a window view looking outside at the larger ringed planet.

Dallas tells them to prepare for disengagement of the smaller towing vehicle from the larger refinery ship. The smaller ship then slides forward on a platform, as the computer Mother gives a countdown that foreshadows the countdown at the film's climax, when Mother, to Ripley's frustration, refuses to reverse the countdown to the ship's auto-destruction. Ripley now announces that the "umbilicus" is clear as the towing ship comes loose and drops away, heading for the planetoid below (note that in Sign Regime A, all gynecological images and metaphors have been "mechanized" and appropriated by Father Science). Dallas then has the engines turned on, and the ship's exhaust ports light up with a yellow glow as it drops and heads for the planetoid. The ship rolls slightly and then drifts, allowing the planet's gravitational field to pull it down.

As they pass through the planetoid's blue-gray atmosphere, the ship hits turbulence and the ride becomes rough. Dallas warns them that there will be a "little bump" as the ship touches down. On C deck, there is a brief shot of Parker and Brett, who hear a screeching sound, indicating that the ship has lost one of its shields, but Dallas continues with the landing anyway.

An exterior shot of the *Nostromo* shows it landing in dense, murky air while its navigation lights come on in luminous, pearlescent rows beneath its belly. Mother starts another countdown as the ship slowly drops like a metallic bird of prey to the rocky, barren surface. The landing is disastrous, however, and a fire breaks out inside the bridge which requires immediate usage of the fire extinguishers. Alarms go off and floodlights turn on inside the smoky bridge while the crew frantically scurry around to put the fire out. Dallas demands that somebody from C deck give him a damage report.

Once the fire is out, Parker's voice can be heard coming through a speaker announcing that they will require "dry dock" in order to fix the damage to the ship.

From C deck below, Parker and Brett are shown standing in smoky blue air with sparks popping and flashing around them as Parker informs the bridge that he and Brett will have to reroute an entire series of ducts and that it will require them 25 hours in which to do so. Ripley's voice then comes over their intercom to inform them that she will soon be arriving down there to check on the damage, while Brett mutters under his breath that she better stay the fuck out of his way. Parker comments, drily, that he'd like to know what she thinks she's going to do once she gets there.

The chaotic landing is the film's first indication of the truly fragile nature of the "absolute world island" which the *Nostromo* constitutes. The hull was not breached and "cabin pressure" was still retained, but surviving onboard a spacecraft is a tentative and potentially very dangerous existence should something go irreversibly wrong. The landing is, of course, an omen of worse things to come.

The scene's vectorial semiotics should be noted, as well, since the detachable tow ship of the *Nostromo* was drawn by artist Ron Cobb to loosely resemble a bird of prey.[28] Indeed, it reminds one of the Indian Garuda bird of Hindu mythology (the Indonesians have even named one of their airlines "Garuda Airlines") which was a solar bird that carried Vishnu on its back. It was so huge that it could pick up elephants in its talons, but its symbology was normally opposed to the earthly, chthonic creatures known as *nagas*, or serpents, which were Garuda's enemies and regarded by him as food.[29]

It should be no surprise then that a mechanical Garuda bird from Sign Regime A will soon encounter a science-fictional equivalent of the Hindu *nagas* inside the derelict spacecraft on the planetoid below, where the floor of the ship contains not only rows of eggs, but also serpent-like designs that are littered across the spaces between the eggs and which are only visible to the carefully discerning eye.[30] The alien itself is simply a transformed serpent with humanoid characteristics (just as the *nagas* were often visualized in Indian art as half-human, half-snake). The serpent, of course, belongs to the earth and to the ancient brood, in Greek myth, of Gaia and her Titan offspring, many of which were associated with serpents (such as Typhon, who was human from the waist up and serpent from the waist down).

Sign Regime B (the Gigerian sign regime) is likewise associated with the earth, the Mother and with Gaia and her brood of monstrous beings which were defeated by Zeus and cast down into Tartaros,[31] a Greek designation of the underworld. Zeus is one of the early incarnations of Father Science who, during the Greek metaphysical age, displaced the matrilineal and matriarchal beings from the former pre-metaphysical age (note that Zeus comes equipped with a paternal womb, for he gives birth to Athena, the goddess of rationality, from out of his own skull).

Alien is all about the rediscovery of precisely the Greek underworld of Gaian Titans by Father Science, the master signifier of Sign Regime A on a turn of the historical spiral 2500 years later. The planetoid with the derelict ship is, in a way, the Greek underworld of Tartaros down to which the *nagas* and Titans have been cast and which the unwary crew of the *Nostromo* inadvertently let loose again.

Excursion

(20:01 – 27:50)

An exterior shot of the nose of the ship now follows, inside which can be glimpsed tiny human occupants moving around while the sound of howling wind from the hostile landscape outside can be heard over the soundtrack.

Inside the ship, on the bridge, Lambert is smoking a cigarette, and Dallas, coffee cup in hand, asks Ash if there is any other response from the distress beacon. Ash tells him that there has been no response and that all other channels are dead. Dallas orders the crew to "kick on the floods," and another exterior shot of the ship now follows with its floodlights coming on in rows while the wind continues to howl around the ship. The floodlights illuminate what appears to be a rocky landscape with bizarre perpendicular rocks jutting up at odd angles everywhere.

Back inside, Kane, Dallas and Ash confer on the bridge, and Kane tells them that they can't go anywhere under such conditions. But Ash points out that Mother has told him the sun is coming up in another twenty minutes, and Dallas inquires how far away they are from the source of the transmission. Ash tells him that they are just under 2,000 meters away, and Kane inquires if that is walking distance. Dallas laughs and then requests Ash to give him the atmospherics, to which Ash replies that it is almost primordial: high concentrations of nitrogen, methane, carbon dioxide, etc. Dallas asks if there is anything else, and Ash tells him that it's mostly lava-based rock and granite, and very, very cold.

Kane volunteers to be in the first group to go out, and then Dallas tells Lambert he wants her along, as well. Lambert does not seem thrilled with the idea, and Dallas says that they better get out the weapons.

In the next scene, Ash is shown zipping up his jumpsuit near his observation blister. He pauses for a moment and then does a quick, bizarre jog in place, as though he might be cold (or, as an android, may already be nearing malfunctionality). Blowing on his enclosed fist, he takes a seat inside his blister.

There follows a shot of Dallas, Lambert and Kane, all suited up inside their spacesuits—designed by the French comic book artist Moebius with a vaguely Japanese samurai warrior feel to them—waiting at the airlock, which then unhooks as two sliding doors open to reveal a spinning floodlight and the sound of terrible winds. This is now a threshold, for they are about to cross over from an absolute world island—sealed off against barren environments--into a landscape of complete hostility toward human existence. The three of them then clamber out onto an elevator platform which then carries them to the ground, while Ash is shown sliding his electric chair into place inside his observation blister.

Lambert insists she can't see a goddamned thing, while Dallas shouts into his comlink to Ash, asking if he is receiving their electronic image feeds. Ash waves down at them with both hands. He tells Dallas that he has good contact on his board and is able to see what they see via his grainy monitor.

Meanwhile, back inside the ship on C Deck, Parker and Brett are standing near a vent that is blowing exhaust loudly, and Parker shouts to Ripley that he would like to ask her a question. He asks whether, if they find what they're looking for out there, that will mean that he and Brett will then get full shares. Ripley, irritated by his rehash of the same conversation over and over, tells him not to worry and that he will get whatever he's got coming to him. Brett threatens a labor strike, and says he's not doing anymore work until they get this straightened out. But Ripley tells him that he is guaranteed by law to receive a share. Mocking her, Parker yells, "What?" and she tells him to fuck off, then strides away. She informs both of them, over her shoulder, that she will be on the bridge if they need her. Laughing, Parker shuts off the valve of steam.

There now follows a shot of the desolate landscape across which Lambert, Kane and Dallas are making their way with great difficulty. Weird vents of steam erupt from the rocks all around them and Lambert reiterates that she can't see anything. Kane tells her to quit griping, and Lambert replies that she likes griping. Dallas, irritated, tells them to knock it off.

Ripley, onboard the ship, slides into her console with a cup of coffee in hand and seats herself in front of her monitors. She flips a few switches and then leans back in her seat, one leg raised, to puzzle over the data.

Next comes an exterior shot of a dim and distant sunrise, which barely illuminates the strange landscape, with its curvilinear and erect rocks. The landscape is the first thing in the movie to appear which has been designed by the artist H.R. Giger and built in a movie studio to his specifications.[32] The three space truckers have now entered the Underworld of Sign Regime B, which is a dark and forbidding place that corresponds to Homeric descriptions of the cold and murky realm of Hades.

As Lambert, Kane and Dallas make their way over a hill, they encounter the film's second Gigerian signifier: the derelict spacecraft that is transmitting the signal. The ship rests on the craggy landscape surrounded by a miasmatic fog: it is a gigantic U-shaped spacecraft the design of which seems to defy logic.

Dallas then asks Ash over his comlink whether he can see what they're seeing and Ash responds by saying that he can, and that he has never seen anything like it. Ash watches through the monitor as Dallas tells him, "This is very bizarre," for the ship appears to be stranger and more bizarre the closer they get to it.

Lambert asks what it could possibly be and then, suddenly frightened, says they should get out of there. But Kane insists that they've come this far, so they may as well investigate it.

To Ash's frustration, the data feeds are becoming glitchy and he asks them to repeat what they just said. But he can no longer hear their voices very well and their monitors are failing as they get closer to the ship, so he tells them he's going back to his console. But the data feed at the console isn't any better, and there follows an exterior shot of the derelict ship from a frontal view as Lambert, Kane and Dallas make their way toward what appears to be three curvilinear entrances. They look like enormous vulvas, and as the three of them prepare to step inside, Ash loses contact with them altogether.

The derelict spacecraft is the first of Giger's compressed signifiers: that is to say, it is a hybrid image that cross-splices and compresses many images together into one fantastic vision. The immediate association is that the ship resembles a giant bone, and indeed, bone was one of Giger's favorite media in which to sculpt. On the set, he requested that hundreds of bones from animals of all kinds be sent to his workshop so that he could design and sculpt both the space jockey that will be found inside the ship and also the mature form of the alien. It is not a cult of the dead, however—for this is a film about the appropriation of the metaphysical vulva by Father Science, so its semiotics are located at the other end, that of the entrance pole to the physical world, not its exit.[33]

The spacecraft also resembles a surrealist version of the ancient Uroboros, the serpent biting its tail that was *the* classic signifier of the pre-metaphysical age, all the way down to the time of Homer, where it occurs in the form of Okeanos, the world-encircling serpent. It is both a temporal and a spatial image, for it connotes the cycle of Eternal Return from the age of the mythical consciousness structure, in which all things ran round in circles, but it also represents the uteromorphic boundaries of an enclosed world, a vision of a flat earth sealed off by the great amniotic oceans. In this scene, Father Science—whose immediate representative is Ash, the ship's science officer—is rediscovering the banished Titans that have been thrown down into the Underworld as a middenheap of signifiers that were inconsistent with the logocentric age. Such signifiers include giants, serpents, Titans, Furies and other similar holdovers from the regime of Mother Right that were cast off and put down by the later generations of Homeric deities like Zeus and Apollo. Indeed, the trial of Orestes, in Aeschylus's *Oresteia*, guilty of matricide, is the last stand of the matriarchy which, forever after, has been excluded from the order of Father Right.[34]

When the three explorers approach the triple entrance of the ship, with its three vulva-like openings—recall David

55

Cronenberg's "trifurcate uterus" in his film *Dead Ringers*—the ship is transformed into a woman with her legs spread apart, for what they will find inside are eggs and a huge dead embryo.

The question is *who* will possess the right to appropriate the metaphysical vulva: Father Science which, with the constructions and creations of his paternal womb, has surrounded and enframed the planet with technical environments that have become increasingly more and more biomorphic in shape—recall Biosphere II or the architectural constructions of Zaha Hadid or Santiago Calatrava—or else, the powers of Gaia herself, who will resist this enframing process with the monstrous titans of her own brood in the form of floods, hurricanes, tsunamis and earthquakes?

Inside the labs of big corporations, Father Science is busy appropriating the biomorphogenetic power to create life artificially with in vitro fertilization, cloning and stem cell research that involves the creation of miniature embryos that are brought into being and then mined for spare parts, while the miniature blastulae are then destroyed.

Alien is a way of exploring these themes by creating a metaphoric scenario that avoids direct confrontation with the themes themselves but unsettles the viewer's subliminal unconscious with the power of its images, for the viewer's unconscious mind knows very well what it is looking at.

Space Jockey
(27:51 – 31:11)

The scene that now follows shows Lambert, Kane and Dallas entering inside the spacecraft, where they encounter strangely curved walls that look as though they had been made out of giant bones and then covered with liquid metal. The impression in the darkened, cavernous interior lit only by the flashlights at the tops of their helmets is the inside of a human ribcage. Kane takes the lead and tells the others that he has found something different further ahead, something with a wall that they might be able to climb. Kane is the first up over the precipice, where he pauses for a moment as he surveys the incredible nature of their discovery, then continues his climb up to the edge of a dais into what appears to be an enormous gallery.

As the camera pans back, the second of Giger's compressed signifiers comes into view: the ancient, dead skeleton of a space giant strapped into his chair at the console of what looks like an enormous telescope. But the telescope, aimed at the ship's dome-shaped oculus, is obviously some sort of navigational tool, and so one presumes that the dead giant must be a space navigator, like the pilots of the Spacing Guild in Frank Herbert's *Dune* novels. Indeed, Giger's space jockey invites a certain comparison with the space navigator that David Lynch's film version of *Dune* opens with: a strange horizontal worm with a huge head which is brought into the throne room of the Emperor Padishah inside of a huge polished black sarcophagus with glass casing on its front end. Herbert's space navigators have the ability to "fold space" using prescient abilities conferred upon them by consuming huge doses of the drug called spice (which also, over time, deforms their bodies into these larval-looking creatures). Giger's space jockey would seem to be a similar sort of entity (and of course, one must not forget that before he was brought in to do the designs for *Alien*, Giger worked on Alejandro Jodorowsky's ill fated *Dune* project).

The jockey is centered in his navigational device upon a large round dais that vaguely resembles an Aztec calendar, and as Dallas steps up onto the navigator's platform for a closer look, he comments that it seems as though the bones of its chest were bent outward from the inside, as though something had exploded out of it. Lambert wonders aloud what happened to the rest of the crew and then, still very much creeped out, reiterates her desire to "get the hell out of here."

Kane then yells for the attention of the other two, for he has found a hole in the ground apparently leading to another level of the ship, its own equivalent, perhaps, to the *Nostromo*'s C Deck. "Let's see what you make of this," he tells Dallas.

As I've mentioned, Giger's space jockey—which was largely constructed by himself at the huge studio where *Alien* was filmed at Elstree in England—is another one of his compressed signifiers that comes with its own built-in meaning cloud. Traces of other signifiers have been gathered and compressed together inside the image itself, as though it came equipped with its own unconscious. In the logocentric age, things are allowed to have only *one* meaning, while all other signifiers are repressed into the etymological trace clouds surrounding the words (which Joyce attempted to archaeologize in *Finnegans Wake*). Unfortunately, I think Scott does some damage to the ambiguity of his own image when he gives an "explanation" for the space jockey in his prequel *Prometheus*, where he explains it away as one of a race of engineers who have created the aliens as bioweapons. It is a bit like Arthur C. Clarke's novelistic sequels to Kubrick's *2001: A Space Odyssey*, in which Clark flattens Kubrick's images out into one-level explanations for the signifiers in Kubrick's film, signifiers that worked so well precisely because the viewer has no idea what they mean and his / her imagination is therefore activated.

Scott also makes the mistake of explaining Giger's dead giant as wearing a "space suit" or exoskeleton that can be put on or taken off by the Engineers. The beauty of the image of the space jockey in *Alien* is precisely that the viewer has no idea *what* the space jockey is—whether it has grown out of its chair by some bizarre feat of genetic engineering or what have you—and so the meaning cloud surrounding the image remains inexhaustible as a result.

One of the other signifiers compressed into Giger's space jockey is that it evokes the myth of the race of giants out of Hesiod's *Theogony*, a race of huge beings who were born as children of the goddess Gaia and who went to war against Zeus, who cast them down into the underworld. There is a missing epic from about the time of Homer entitled *The Gigantomachia* that would have detailed the specifics of this war.

But the larger metanarrative framing that myth is that the ancients saw themselves as having been preceded by an Age of Giants, huge men who must have been strong enough to move the giant stone blocks which they used to assemble the architecture of the palaces at Mycenae, Pylos and Tiryns. The Greeks therefore regarded themselves as devolved and miniaturized from an earlier generation of giants, and many of their best scholars—men such as Pliny the Elder—insisted that the bones of giants like Orion had been dug up as proof of the existence of such a race of beings (whereas most of these bones were from the skeletons of dwarf elephants and other extinct fauna). Empedocles, for instance, claimed that the skull of an extinct dwarf elephant, with a huge hole in the middle of its head, was physical proof of the prior existence of the Cyclops from *The Odyssey*.[35]

There is also a sort of hidden reference to H.P. Lovecraft's novel *At the Mountains of Madness*, wherein an Arctic expedition finds an ancient civilization buried deep in the mountains of Antarctica. Inside the cyclopean interiors of the cities of this ancient race, the narrators discover, to their horror, that some of the beings, known as shoggoths, are still living and prowling through the gloomy corridors of the ancient city.

There is also the semiotic possibility that, since the crew have gone inside the vulvular entrance of the derelict ship that resembles--from one point of view, anyway--a woman with her legs spread apart, that they have discovered a sort of dead embryo, fossilized inside of its uteromorphic chamber, a huge round cavern. The semiotics of the ship's interior, after all, are entirely female: there is not a straight line to be found anywhere, and perspectively correct space simply does not exist on the inside of this ship. It is a uteromorphic container, just as the ancient Uroboros was a uteromorphic world disc that encircled, and enclosed, the earth.

Indeed, Kane, Lambert and Dallas have entered inside what theoretician Peter Sloterdijk calls "a negative gynecology," where they have discovered such "nobjects" as fetuses, vaginal walls, cervical entrances and a dead embryo ("nobjects" according to Sloterdijk are what the fetus, not yet a subject, registers inside the womb around it, such as the placenta, sounds from outside the mother's body, the uterine walls, etc. In other words, they are not yet *quite* "objects" because there is not yet *quite* a subjective consciousness to perceive them. Hence, they are registered as "non-objects," or "nobjects" for short).[36]

In any event, it is the realm of the Mothers which the three explorers have stumbled onto: an underworld of cast-off signifiers forgotten by the logocentric age of linear meaning.

Eggs
(31:12 – 35:33)

Meanwhile, back aboard the ship, Ripley has been observing data regarding the distress signal and she contacts Ash on her intercom to inform him that Mother has deciphered part of the signal and that it doesn't look like an S.O.S., but rather a warning. Ripley says that she is going to go out after Kane, Lambert and Dallas, but Ash asks her what the point would be since by the time it would take her to reach them, they would already know whether the signal was a warning or not.

Back inside the derelict ship, Kane is in process of being lowered into the cargo hold using a tripod and a wench. Dallas asks him if he sees anything down there and Kane replies that it looks like some sort of a cave. There follows a shot—it is an old-fashioned matte painting--that shows just how gigantic the cave is, for it seems to recede into the distance for miles. (This would have been the sequence in which a second structure was to have been found, a pyramid or egg-silo through the top of which Kane was to have been lowered.)

Kane eventually reaches the bottom, where a series of metallic partitions have divided up the ship's cargo hold, which is filled with thousands of alien eggs. Kane informs

Dallas that there is some sort of thin blue mist covering the eggs which reacts when broken. Kane then slips and falls from the metal transom down amongst the eggs. Dallas inquires whether he is all right, and Kane tells him that he's fine, he just slipped.

Kane then approaches one of the eggs, which has a kind of leathery quality about it. As he looks closer, it appears that tiny droplets are falling from the egg *upwards* in a bizarre defiance of gravity. Kane informs Dallas that the egg appears to be completely sealed, but it makes a sudden hissing noise and the camera pans down to show something faintly luminous stirring within it. Weapon in hand, Kane leans carefully forward and tells Dallas that there is something moving inside the egg, then backs up slightly as its four petals open with a hissing sound. Unable to contain his curiosity, Kane leans forward again to peer at the organic insides of the egg, which Ridley Scott had filled with real animal organs, such as sheep's guts.

As he peers into the rather uterine-looking contents of the egg, a creature with a whip-lash tail for a spring darts up at his faceplate and knocks him backwards.

An exterior shot of the ship looking cold and ghostly in the fog then follows.

Eggs, of course, have a female valency and they are part of the Gigerian Sign Regime, but they are also associated with less evolved and earlier forms of terrestial and amphibial life. Fish, amphibians, crustaceans, insects and reptiles all lay eggs and these were the earliest complex creatures to colonize the waters and then eventually the land of the earth. Mammals coevolved with the dinosaurs, appearing as early as the Triassic, but they probably still laid eggs until the development of placental mammals sometime near the end of the Cretaceous. As Peter Sloterdijk once put it in an interview, the evolutionary development of the female womb was the world's first apartment and therefore its first microsphere.[37] (Microspheres, as Sloterdijk defines them in his book *Spheres I: Bubbles*, are always formed by a minimum of two entities in dyadic interaction with one another).

Kane, however, has become infected with an ancient, less evolved type of creature with an exoskeleton that still lays eggs. The egg-laying reptiles, insects and crustaceans are part of the brood of Gaia that was thrust down into the underworld by Zeus, just as the dinosaurs were scaled down and miniaturized by the catastrophe that wiped them out and allowed them to survive only in the lesser form of snakes, lizards, birds and crocodiles, while the days of the mammalian regime—which thus far has led to their completely encircling the earth and placing it inside of a techno-sphere—then overshadowed them.

In *Alien*, eggs are dangerous, for they carry inside them the brood of Gaia's Titans which are now about to be transferred from one sign regime—the Gigerian—to another, that of the inside of a completely mechanized absolute world island. The penetration of a mechanized world island like the *Nostromo* by Gaian creatures is tantamount to an irruption and rebellion of the monsters of the underworld from the *inside* of the techno-scientific realm of Sign Regime A. Unleashed from the canvases of Bosch—which are full of eggs, by the way—and up from the underworld created by Milton in his *Paradise Lost*, in which he places the entire pantheon of the deities of pagan antiquity, the metaphysical age with its mental consciousness structure will now be tasked with containing a very dangerous biohazard that is self-organizing, reproduces rapidly, and defies the attempts of technology to contain it.

The absolute world island of the *Nostromo* is about to become a "maximal stress environment" in which the mechanical womb supplied by the ship's maternal computer will no longer be sufficient to maintain optimal safe living conditions.

The question thus becomes, which regime is stronger: that of Father Science, together with his tools that mimic life with artificial conditions; or Mother Right, with her serpentine abominations that display a reproductive life force that not even science can contain or convincingly imitate?

Face-Hugger
(35:34 – 42:43)

In the next scene, Ash is shown anxiously awaiting the arrival of Lambert, Dallas and Kane from their excursion. The moment he sees them approaching through the storm, he heads for the air lock.

The outside elevator carries the three up to the air-lock, where Dallas asks if Ripley is available on his com-link. Ash goes to the air lock and informs Ripley that he is there waiting, to which she replies, "Right." Inside the air lock the three explorers are shown with vents of steam blowing over them for decontamination purposes. Dallas informs Ripley that they're now clean and tells her to let them in, but first she wants to know what has happened to Kane. Dallas explains that something has attached itself to him and that they must get him to the infirmary immediately. Ripley cautiously asks what kind of thing has attached itself to Kane, but Dallas shouts back at her that it is some kind of an organism and orders her to open the hatch. Ripley tells him that there is a great risk to the ship if they let Kane in, and that quarantine procedures require twenty-four hours for decontamination. Dallas says that Kane might not live for another twenty-four hours, to which Ripley replies—correctly, as it turns out—that if they break quarantine procedures then everyone onboard could die. Lambert then yells at Ripley to open the hatch, but she maintains a firm "no." Dallas specifies, however, that he is giving her a direct order to open the hatch, but she still refuses. Ash, waiting anxiously in front of the doors of the lock, decides to override Ripley and presses the button to open it, then informs Ripley that the inner hatch has been opened.

The next shot is a close-up of Kane's helmet through which the creature has managed to melt its way inside. Ash is in the middle of cutting the helmet open using a laser scalpel and together he and Dallas—inside the autodoc now—pull the two halves of the helmet away to reveal yet another of Giger's compressed signifiers. "My God," Dallas says when he sees the yellowish organism that has completely covered Kane's face and has wrapped a serpentine tail around his neck, which it tightens, threatening to kill him. The creature is a sort of compression of an arachnid with a crustacean and has legs that look more like long human fingers than spider's legs. In either case, it is clearly exoskeletal in nature.

Dallas, holding half of Kane's helmet, asks Ash what the hell it is that they're looking at.

Meanwhile, in the corridor outside the autodoc, Lambert, Parker and Brett watch the entire operation through a glass window. Brett asks the same question that Dallas has just asked Ash, rhetorically, while Parker then asks how the hell Kane could be breathing with that thing on his face? Parker is in the middle of asking why they don't just freeze Kane when Ripley comes down the stairwell behind them. She is furious, and Lambert immediately turns upon her and calls her a bitch, while giving her a full, and vicious, slap in the face.[38] Parker and Brett run over to break up the feud, while Lambert accuses Ripley of having left them out there to die in the air lock.

Dallas then yells from the other side of the autodoc and tells Ripley that when he gives an order, he expects it to be obeyed. Ripley counters by asking him: even if it's against the law? To which Dallas, unhesitatingly replies, "You're goddammned right!"

Parker then leans forward and yells through the glass to Dallas that maybe Ripley has a point, since they have no idea what that thing on Kane's face is.

Inside the autodoc, meanwhile, Dallas is asking Ash how they're going to remove the creature from Kane's face. Ash tells him to hold on a minute while he grabs a pair of forceps and then tries to use them to pull one of the creature's fingers away, but this only has the result of tightening the snake-like coil around Kane's neck. Dallas tells him that the creature is not coming off without tearing Kane's whole face off with it. Ash suggests that they take a look inside of him.

Ash then walks over to the X-ray unit and punches a few buttons that cause Kane's platform to swivel round inside of it, while a glass partition closes him in. Ash tells Dallas that he can now take his protective mask off.

There follows a shot of a scanning device that creates an X-ray image of Kane as it slides along the length of the unit from head to toe. Looking at the X-ray, Dallas notices that the creature has inserted something down Kane's throat, which Ash suggests that it is using to feed him oxygen. Dallas wonders aloud why the creature would paralyze him, put him into a coma and then keep him alive. The whole thing is a puzzle, but he insists that they have to cut it off Kane's face no matter what. Ash interjects that they should not be too hasty here, since the creature is, after all, feeding him oxygen and if they remove it, it could kill him. But Dallas says he'll accept full responsibility for whatever happens.

There follows a shot in which they have removed Kane from the X-ray machine and put him back where he was. Dallas asks Ash how he wants to go about doing this, and Ash tells him that he will use the laser scalpel to make an incision just above one of the creature's knuckles. But when he applies the laser scalpel to one of the creature's fingers, a jet of yellow blood shoots out onto the floor and eats a hole right through it.

Dallas is worried that the acid-blood may eat through the hull, and so he runs out, while the crew follows him to the next level down. By the time they get there, though, the acid has dropped through to the next deck, and they chase it down one level further. When it has reached C Deck, the blood has lost its momentum and left a hole in the ceiling. Ripley says that it looks like it's stopping and Parker tells Brett to come take a look at the acid. Dallas asks for a pen from him, which he grabs and then uses to prod the hole. When he pulls it out the pencil is smoking.

Dallas says that he's never seen anything like it except molecular acid, which Brett points out that it must be using for blood. Parker comments that it has a wonderful defense mechanism and that they don't dare kill it.

Ripley then asks about Kane as Dallas hands the ruined pencil back to Brett. Dallas tells them that he will leave Kane to Ash and that Parker and Brett should get back to work on repairing the ship so that they can take off.

The semiotics of this sequence are complex, but there are basically two processes going on, for whenever one sign regime begins to overcode another sign regime, the result is not only a hybridization of the two, but a hybridization that takes place through parallel processes which Deleuze and Guattari in their book *A Thousand Plateaus* call "facialization" and "reterritorialization." [39]

Every sign regime carries its own brand of facialization. For instance the face, in the Hebrew sign regime, is always turned away or hidden: one is not allowed to look upon the visage of God, or even Moses, who has to wear a veil over his face after his confrontation with the deity on Mount Sinai. During the Byzantine age, however, the Roman burial portrait is transformed and reterritorialized into the *en face* visage of "the average white man," who normally turns out to be a saint or one of the other holy entities in the Christian canon. During the later metaphysical age, when the Byzantine icon painting tradition entered into Europe, the saints were pushed out and refacialized as the classic portrait study, usually of a wealthy patron or donor.

With the rise of Modernist art at the end of the nineteenth century, another facialization process began to overcode the previous one of classical art, one which—and this is especially epitomized by Picasso—took the portrait study and broke it into pieces in order to reassemble it as an "integral" visage, or multi-perspectival image. With the post-integral, or postmodern age, however, the portrait—as in the paintings of Francis Bacon, let's say—became what Peter Sloterdijk calls a *detrait*, in which all the signifying features were scrambled, but not to produce an integral image with specific significations, but rather an *a*-signifying visage that meant nothing at all.[40]

In the present instance, as the Gigerian sign regime begins to penetrate and overcode Sign Regime A, it starts precisely by refacialization. Kane's recognizable facial features are simply wiped clean and covered over by a creature with mythic significations that point back to the ancient past of the Titans banished to the underworld during the rise of the mental consciousness structure. The new facialization simply wipes the slate clean and we are given the portrait study of "Face Covered by a Monster."

The alien may be enigmatic to the crew, but it is most definitely teleological. It has a purpose, for related to the metaphysical process of facialization, there is also the process of reterritorialization. When Christian names, for instance, were given by the Spaniards to Native American landmarks, that is an example of "reterritorialization." In other words, a signifier that was once used to signify one thing, is now overcoded and used to signify something else altogether.

Thus, in Sign Regime B, Kane's mouth is reterritorialized as a vagina, while his stomach is reterritorialized as a uterus. If, as Deleuze and Guattari point out, the human hand is simply a deterritorialized paw, while the mouth, originally territorialized for nourishment, is later reterritorialized by the human frontal lobe for the instrument of language, then we can also say that Sign Regime B is using Kane's body to make a new somatic map for itself, a kind of alien cartography that has new significations which anathematize and draw an "X" over the previous bodily organs.

A hybrid regime is thus in process of being created, and the end result in the film will be the creation of a *third* sign regime, a Sign Regime C that is the product of the fusion of the previous two, in imitation of the Hegelian process of thesis, antithesis, synthesis.

When the metaphysical age of the Greeks and the Hebrews overcoded the sign regime of the pre-metaphysical—or mythical—sign regime, the Father appropriated the creative powers of the Mother Goddess. Specifically, he internalized and recoded her womb to serve the uterine function of giving birth to the Logos, or the Word. Hence, Christ incarnates the Word made flesh that is breathed by God down into the virgin womb of Mary, which He uses as a proxy, although he had already demonstrated at the beginning of the Book of Genesis that Adam had appropriated the womb in the side of his body, from which he had given birth to Eve.

In a strange way, the alien is caricaturizing the masculinist appropriation of the metaphysical vulva in the age of Father Science, who imitates her creative powers through laboratory processes like in vitro fertilization, cloning and stem cell research. Note that the alien is planting a tiny embryo inside of Kane's stomach: it is not using sperm to fertilize an egg, since Kane has no eggs to fertilize. The process is morphologically parallel with in vitro fertilization, when a sperm and an egg are incubated in a laboratory to form an embryo, which is *then* carefully inserted into a woman's uterus with a long cylindrical mechanical device. The alien is doing precisely the same thing: it is inserting an already formed tiny embryo into Kane's stomach, which will grow and grow into a serpentine creature that bursts forth from within him, like a man giving birth.

Thus, the image is not, as I would put it, metaphysically "clean." It is composed of signifiers from both Sign Regime A and Sign Regime B to produce a hybridized image out of both regimes, for it is in process of creating a *new* sign regime that is half mythical and half metaphysical-scientific.

Confrontations
(42:44 – 51:43)

Parker and Brett are now shown back at work, soldering the elements of some blown-out mechanical part of the ship's engines on C Deck. Brett tells Parker to "try it," and when he does, has no success. Brett is frustrated that his "fix" didn't take.

Brett then says that he feels like they've been on the planetoid for a whole month, while Parker, agreeing, says that they should never have landed there in the first place. Parker then adds that the sooner they can get everything patched up, the sooner they can get off the planetoid, which gives him the creeps.

The next scene takes place inside the infirmary, where Kane, still with the creature attached to his face, is laid out like a mummy being prepared for burial. The infirmary is dark and quiet, and the camera creeps slowly around to the corner to show Ash at work studying the creature's cells through his microscope and video monitor, when Ripley suddenly comes up behind him and asks him what he thinks it is. Ash, perturbed, tells her he doesn't yet know and then shuts off his monitor and asks her what she wants.

Seating herself on his stool, she says that she would like to have a little talk with him and proceeds by asking about

Kane, to which Ash replies that his condition is stable, with no changes. Then she asks about "our little guest," and Ash, being evasive, says that he's still collating data but that he has confirmed that the creature has an outer layer of protein polysaccharides and that it has a funny habit of shedding its cells and replacing them with polarized silicon, making it one tough little son of a bitch. In an accusing tone, Ripley then says, "and you let him in." Ash defends himself by saying that he was obeying a direct order, but Ripley reminds him that when Dallas and Kane are off the ship, *she* is in command. He tells her that he forgot about that, and she further accuses him of forgetting about the science division's quarantine law. He tells her he didn't forget that at all, but this gives her the opportunity to accuse him of breaking it.

Ash, nettled, puts one hand on his hip and asks her what *she* would have done about Kane since she must've known very well that his only chance of survival was to get him into the infirmary. She says that by breaking quarantine law, however, Ash has put everyone's lives at risk. He suggests that maybe he should've just left Kane outside, and that perhaps he did indeed jeopardize everyone, but that it was a risk he was willing to take. She tells him that's an extraordinary risk to take for a mere science officer. He tries to end the conversation by telling her that she just needs to do her job while he does his.

Thus, the two characters have drawn their boundaries with each other, but the scene has already set the viewer up for the confrontation that will later take place between them when Ash tries to kill her.

There follows an exterior shot of the ship's shuttle, the *Narcissus*, inside which Dallas is shown relaxing while listening to classical music. Ash interrupts him via com-link and tells him that he needs to come have a look at Kane.

Dallas inquires whether the situation is serious, but Ash merely says that it's "interesting." Dallas then gets on the intercom and tells Ripley to meet him in the infirmary right away.

The next shot shows Kane's face completely missing its alien signifier. Ripley's voice can be heard asking what happened to the creature and Ash telling her that he has no idea but that they need to try and find it.

Ash, Dallas and Ripley then carefully enter the gloomy infirmary, looking all about them for the creature. As the three begin tip-toeing around, Ripley warns Dallas to be careful. Ripley bends down and glances beneath the infirmary table upon which Kane has been laid out, while Dallas startles her by causing an object to fall over. Light probe in hand, he is searching up in the corners. Ripley looks in the areas above the autodoc while Ash thinks to close the sliding doors of the infirmary behind them.

Ash, with a light probe and a plastic tray in one hand is looking up in the niches of the ceiling when he notices Ripley poking around in the corner above his monitor and warns her not to look in the corners without a light probe. Ripley then wanders over to examine Kane, while Ash pokes up in the corner that she had been checking, using his light probe.

Ripley says Kane's name, as though to try and wake him up just as the creature's long tail drops down from the ceiling behind her and the creature itself then falls upon her shoulder, to which she reacts by screaming and tossing it to the floor. Dallas protectively covers her on the floor while Ash rushes to the creature and asks where it was. Dallas gestures vaguely that it was "up there somewhere."

He then tells Ash to cover the damn thing, but Ash pokes at it with his light probe and it gives one last dying jolt of its limbs, which Ash explains is just a reflex. He then says, excitedly, that they've got to have a closer look at the creature.

In the next shot, the alien is carefully laid out upon an examining table with its underside belly up. There is no protective covering to its internal organs, which are clearly visible and exposed to Ash's probing with his various instruments.

A debate then follows as the three of them examine the creature and Ash announces that it is obviously dead, to which Ripley replies by saying that they ought to get rid of it. Ash then tells her that this a spectacular scientific finding that has to be taken back to earth and all sorts of tests have to be run on it. Ripley points out that the creature bled acid and that they have no idea what it's going to do when it's dead, but Ash assures her that it's safe to assume that it is not a zombie. Then he turns to Dallas and asks for a decision. Dallas is reluctant but he tells Ash that it's his decision since he's the science officer. Ripley, incredulous, pursues him out the corridor.

As he walks away he tells her he's not going to change his mind, but she tells him she's not trying to change his mind, she just wants him to listen to her. She hits the button on a door that closes in front of him, forcing him to turn round and face her. Their confrontation has the familiarity about it of a couple, and indeed there are subtle clues and hints throughout the film that the two have been in a relationship at some point along their travels.

She wants to know how he can leave that kind of a decision up to Ash, and Dallas tells her, irritated, that his job is just to run the ship and that anything that has to do with the science division leaves Ash with the final word. Ripley asks him how that happens, and he tells her that it happens that way because it's the way the company wants it to happen. She asks him since when that has been standard procedure and he clarifies by saying that standard procedure is to do whatever the company tells you to do.

Dallas then asks what's going on with the repairs and Ripley tells him that they are mostly finished. He asks why the hell she didn't tell him so in the first place, and she says that there are still a few minutiae left to attend to, such as the reserve power system. He tells her that's all a bunch of horseshit and that they can take off without any of that, but she asks whether that's a good idea. Dallas tells her that he just wants to get the hell off the planetoid.

Now the significance of this little cluster of scenes—which is composed of two confrontations: one between Ripley and Ash and one between Ripley and Dallas—is the gradually rising assertion of Ripley's power as a character. Prior to landing on the planetoid, Dallas had been portrayed as the "man in charge," since he is the ship's captain, after all, but Ripley's decision to leave Kane in quarantine turns out, in retrospect, to have been the correct decision. She fights with both Ash and Dallas to assert the rationality and logic of her decision-making, while, as the story unfolds, it tends to prove her right at every point and the decisions of both Dallas and Ash wrong. Ash, of course, has been assigned by Weyland-Yutani—the ship's owners—to protect the alien at all costs (note that the company's symbol is a variation on the Egyptian winged falcon, thereby assigning the ship a valency of Transcendence: the escape into artificiality and the false transcendence of science and technology, which seeks to replace the mother, her body and the earth at every step).

In other words, once the signifiers from Sign Regime B start to enter into those of Sign Regime A and begin to hybridize in order to create a third sign regime, Ripley's power slowly rises in direct proportion as the viewer begins to realize that the narrative is centered upon *her* and not the other characters. Sign Regime B—the Gigerian regime—belongs to the realm of the Mothers and their ancient matriarchal powers, and it is no coincidence that the arrival of those signifiers onboard the ship takes place in tandem with the rise of Ripley's power as a decision-maker.

It is as though the ancient matriarchal-matrilineal sign regime signified by the alien actually strengthens and gives power to Ripley as the central (matriarchal) protagonist and dragon-slayer. It is *she* who will destroy the beast, not the men.

Chest Burster

(51:44 – 57:44)

There now follows an exterior shot of the ship slowly and ponderously lifting its way off the planetoid. Parker and Brett, strapped into their seats, warn of engine over-heating and Parker then tells Brett to spit on it for two minutes. Ripley's voice can be heard over the intercom saying that the ship is hot and getting hotter. It is a difficult take off for this damaged mechanical Garuda bird.

Ripley, strapped into her seat, informs the crew that she is engaging the artificial gravity and altering the vectors. The ship does nevertheless manage to escape the gravitational well of the planetoid, and Parker pridefully says that when he and Brett fix something, then it stays fixed.

There follows a shot of the mother ship to which they have now, presumably, docked.

The next scene is an interior shot in an alcove of the mess hall in which Brett is rolling a cigarette while Ripley sits beside him, and Dallas and Parker are across from them. Parker is voicing the opinion that he thinks they ought to freeze Kane, since if he has a disease that would make the most sense. Brett then says, "right," and Ripley points out that whenever Parker says something, Brett always says "right" back to him. To which Brett replies: "Right." Ripley then asks Parker what he thinks about his sidekick following him around saying "right" all the time just like a regular parrot. Parker laughs and tells Brett to shape up. Dallas, who always seems to be in a bad mood, tells them all to knock it off and that Kane is simply going to have to go into quarantine. Ripley says that they will, too, in any event.

Lambert walks in and offers some news to lower their spirits. Dallas tells her to let him have it: Lambert then announces that they have ten more months to go until they arrive at earth.

Ash's voice then comes over the intercom and tells Dallas that he needs to come have a look at Kane. Dallas asks if his condition has worsened, but Ash insists that it is simpler if he just comes and sees him.

The next shot is a view of Kane in the infirmary, awake and sitting up while the rest of the crew surround him and ask him how he's doing. Parker, specifically, asks him how he feels, to which Kane replies that he is doing just terrific, next silly question, please. Dallas asks him if he remembers anything about the planetoid, while Ripley leans forward and asks him what's the last thing he *does* remember. Kane seems to have difficulty, but he says that he seems to remember having some horrible dream about smothering. Anyway, he continues, where are we?

Ripley tells him that they're on their way home, and Brett says that it's time to go back to the freezerinos. Everyone smiles, but Kane insists that he must have something to eat before going back to the freezers. Parker agrees that he needs something to eat, too, and so does everyone else. Dallas announces that they will then have another meal before bedtime and that he is buying.

The next shot takes place in the mess hall as a kind of Last Supper homage which shows all seven crewmembers seated at the table with food spread out before them. Kane is heaping food from a bowl onto his plate and says that the first thing he is going to do when he gets back home is to get some decent food. Parker, seated beside him, tells him that he can dig that, although he's eaten worse food before, but also better. Lambert, across the table, tells Parker that he pounds down the stuff like there's no tomorrow. Parker says, with a lascivious grin, that right now he'd rather be eating something else, but for the time being he's thinking of food. The reference to cunnilingus causes Lambert to blush slightly, although she also smiles as she flicks ashes from her cigarette. Kane then chimes in that at least, in that case, he knows what "it's" made of, but Parker says he doesn't want to talk about what "it's" made of while he's eating.

At this point, Kane begins choking and Parker asks him what's wrong and insists that the food couldn't be that bad. Dallas asks if he's choking on his food, but it is clearly something much more serious as Kane stands up, clutching his sides in agony and begins to go into convulsions.

Ash, watching quietly from across the table, realizes that Kane must be having a seizure and reaches over to put a spoon into his mouth to prevent him from biting off his tongue. Kane, lying on top of the table, thrashes about while Parker tries to force the spoon into Kane's mouth.

Kane is now screaming, and then suddenly a red burst of blood erupts from his chest, staining his white T-shirt with a crimson splash. This startles everyone, for they have no idea what is going on. There is a pause for a second and then the alien creature punches its way through Kane's torso in a fountain of blood that sprays everywhere, squirting Lambert in particular. The creature, about the size of a cobra, peers around at its surroundings, while Parker raises a knife at it but is stopped by Ash who insists that he dare not touch it. The creature then gives forth its newborn cry with glittering silver teeth and then races across the table and disappears before anyone even has a chance to process the horror that they have just witnessed.

In the metaphysical age, as I've already pointed out, it is the Father who appropriates the metaphysical vulva from the Great Mother: Zeus gives birth to Athena from his head with the aid of an axe that is supplied by the smith god Hephaestus (shown below), who chops open his head to release Athena, who had been planted inside his skull in the first place through a similar conception by mouth when Zeus devoured Metis and her child because an oracle had told him that one of her children would overthrow his rule.[41] Adam, in the Book of Genesis, likewise, gives birth to Eve from out of his side, and God himself gives birth to the Logos as Christ, breathed forth by proxy into the womb of Mary.

In the famous chest burster scene of *Alien*, the semiotics are mixed because what Kane gives birth to from his stomach—reterritorialized as a uterus—is not a creature, like Athena, of rationality and wisdom, or human decency, such as Eve, the first woman, but rather one of Gaia's titans, a serpent-like creature that they have picked up from their sojourn in the underworld of repressed signifiers excluded from the rational structures—such as perspectival space, built using a Cartesian grid—of the metaphysical age. The mechanical Garuda bird has picked up a *naga* from the underworld, which is now running around loose inside of an absolute mechanical world island that has been constructed by Father Science specifically to keep such beings *out*— and here, one needs to be reminded that the symbol of the Weyland-Yutani company is an adaptation of the outspread wings of Horus, the falcon god. Both regimes, then, have opposed signifiers, for the bird and the snake have been semiotic opposites throughout the entire history of mythology, going as far back, at least, as Mesopotamia.

The unleashing of a *naga* on the inside of an absolute world island automatically transforms the artificial safety and security provided by this substitute for Gaia—a computer named Mother—into a maximal stress zone, in which one must now fight for one's survival against a hostile "other."

If a single thing goes wrong inside of an absolute world island—an O ring, say, that freezes and cracks during take-off; or a two pound piece of foam rubber that gains enough velocity to punch a hole in the tiles of a space shuttle— then a chain reaction sets in which can lead to the inevitable destruction of that world island.

Now the crew of the *Nostromo* must unite in a form of

maximal stress cooperation (Heiner Muhlmann's phrase)—like the Greeks against the Persians at Marathon, say; or the Maccabees against the Seleucids—to expel an alien being that serves as a mortal threat to them all. Otherwise, the artificial macrosphere of the industrial environment that protects them will disintegrate.

Epidermis
(57:45 – 1:08:17)

There follows a brief shot of crewmembers searching through the ship's corridors for the creature. Dallas asks them if they've seen anything, to which they reply that they haven't. The ship is huge and its corridors are dark, poorly lit and labyrinthine. The creature could be anywhere.

Next comes a shot of the crew gathered on the bridge before a video monitor on one of the consoles showing Kane's dead body wrapped like a mummy. Dallas, seated at the console, tells them that the inner hatch is now sealed and glumly asks if anybody wishes to say anything. There is a pause, since no one knows what to say, and so Dallas then reaches forward to punch a button that ejects Kane's mummified body out of the ship and into the dark abysses of deep space, where it goes flipping, end over end until it tumbles from view.

There is then a shot of the *Nostromo* floating silently through space like a miniature city, an absolute world island that has now been transformed by an escaped signifier into a maximal stress zone.

The next scene has the crew gathered around a table displaying the weapons which they will use to capture the escaped creature. Brett holds up a long metallic stick and explains that it is just a prod, like an ordinary cattle prod, but that the one thing you don't want to do is get your hand near it. He demonstrates by poking the ceiling with it, and electric sparks shoot out in reaction. He tells them that it shouldn't damage the creature, unless its skin is thicker than theirs, but it should give it some incentive. Brett is here in the role of the ancient blacksmith god, Hephaestus or Vulcan, who provides the ruling warrior gods with their weapons, just as the Kyklopes in Hesiod's *Theogony* make the thunderbolts that Zeus will use in his war against the giants and titans.[42]

Lambert then points out that all they now have to do is find the alien, but Ash says that he's taken care of that by designing a special tracking device. He says that one just sets it to search for a moving object and turns it on, but points out that it hasn't got much of a range. Ripley asks what it keys off of, and Ash, once again seeming irritated with her, says that it responds to micro changes in air density. Dallas reaches for it and tells Ash to give him a demo, and while Dallas is holding the gadget, Ash passes his hand in front of it, causing it to make an electronic sound as he does so.

Dallas then divides them into two teams: he will go with Ash and Lambert, while Ripley takes Parker and Brett. He further explains to Parker, who is nervously chewing gum, that he doesn't want any heroics out of him. Dallas then explains that the creature will be captured by the net that Parker is holding and that it will then be put into the airlock. He further states that all communication channels on all decks will be open, so he expects to be updated frequently.

The scene then changes to Ripley leading Parker and

Brett on C deck, holding a large flashlight while navigating through one of its extremely narrow, octagonal corridors. She mentions to Parker and Brett that she thought they told her they had fixed 12 module, to which Brett replies that they did and that he doesn't understand why it's now gone dark. Parker then suggests that the circuits must have burned out.

Parker takes a moment to rewire a panel that causes the circuits to come back on, and the grimy fluorescent lighting flickers back into being. Meanwhile, Ripley, holding Ash's tracking device, has begun to pick up a signal and she motions for them to follow her. They come to a closed gray door with a checkerboard pattern that then slides open to reveal a storage room flooded through the open doorway with grainy blue lighting. Ripley hesitantly enters the room and tells them that the device is indicating that the creature is somewhere within five meters of them. The room is full of discarded space suits and stacks of shipping boxes that have been sitting in the darkness and quietly rusting away for a long time. They approach a series of orange storage lockers where the signal grows stronger and Ripley whispers to Parker that she has found the creature inside one of the lockers. Parker steps forward with the net, while Ripley holds the cattle prod, Brett beside her holding the other end of the net. She tells Parker to wait for her say and when she does so, Parker opens the locker to reveal the ship's cat, Jones, which hisses at them and then runs through the net, past Brett, who does nothing to try and stop it. Ripley yells at him not to let it go, and Parker shouts at him in frustration for letting the cat get past him.

Brett explains to them that it was only the cat, but Parker points out that Brett shouldn't have let it go because now they might pick it up on the tracker again. Brett volunteers to go and find it.

In the next shot, Brett enters a large warehouse-type of open space illuminated with slats of gold and copper-colored light. It appears to be a storage room for outdoor excursion vehicles, and Brett wanders through the huge space calling after the cat. He stops for a moment, seeming to hear some movement up above in the rafters, and continues calling the cat's name, but hears no reply. But then he catches a glimpse of the cat scurrying about in the guts of some excursion vehicle or land rover and chases it round to the other side. He watches the cat scuttle into another room and is just about to go after it, when he notices something strange on the metallic floor and bends down to pick it up. It is a rice-paper thin piece of what looks like snakeskin that has been shed. Brett holds it up with two fingers, puzzled, then drops it and continues his pursuit of the cat into the next room.

The camera then follows his point of view through a narrow opening into a room that is gloomier and grimier and also somewhat smaller. It appears to be a room for repairing vehicles by hoisting them up on a platform like in an auto-mechanic's shop, with chains dangling from the ceiling that are stirred in a faint breeze that makes them rattle like windchimes. The camera pans up to look at the loading unit, which hangs from the ceiling like a huge mechanical claw. Two rectangular openings in the ceiling above allow blue light to come filtering through with water dripping from somewhere in steady streams falling down like rain. As the chains tinkle, it is a bizarre effect, as though a Japanese zen master had designed the entire edifice.

Brett wanders in, looking for the cat, and stands for a moment beneath the refreshing water, removing his baseball cap to allow the cool liquid to dribble across his face as though he had stumbled upon a natural mountain spring waterfall inside of some strange mechanical landscape. As the chains continue tinkling, the camera catches a glimpse of the fully-grown alien hanging upside down amongst them, swaying as though in a breeze. The creature is scarcely distinguishable from any of the other mechanical parts dangling from the ceiling and so Brett doesn't notice it.

Brett then replaces his baseball cap and spots the cat, crouching in a corner. Brett, too, crouches and tries using a soft voice to coax it out from the corner, while the chains dangle in the air behind him. For a moment, the cat seems reassured and starts to come forward, but then when the alien's tail drops down among the chains behind Brett, it hisses. Brett stands up, and as he does so, the creature drops down in a blur behind him, unfolding its body like a piece of mechanical origami. The camera catches a close-up shot of its smooth, crescent-shaped head, glistening with slime and saliva that is dripping from its tooth-infested jaws.

Jones continues to growl and back away, and Brett now realizes that there is something behind him and turns round and looks up, astonished at the monstrosity that is dangling from the ceiling above him. He stands for a moment, as though hypnotized, but the creature leaps forward like a cobra and shoots its toothed-tongue into his skull, crushing his head as it grabs him and he screams as it springs back up with the dangling chains somewhere into the machinery above.

Ripley and Parker, hearing Brett's screams, arrive too late and look up to see only blood dripping down with the water. There is no sign of either Brett or the alien that has made off with him.

The mature version of the alien in this sequence was taken directly from a painting done by H.R. Giger (entitled *Necronom IV*) in his 1976 art book *Necronomicon*, which screenwriter Dan O'Bannon gave to Ridley Scott, and when Scott saw the painting, (which looks remarkably similar to the finished design of the creature in the film), he knew that he had found his monster.[43]

Giger's book is filled with biomechanical images of living, sentient beings which have been captured and seamlessly woven into industrial machinery. In looking at these paintings, which are uniformly gray, one does not know where the flesh ends and where mechanical-industrial parts begin. It is a nightmarish vision of the capture of the human soul by science, and of the overcoding of biology by the sign regime of industrialization. Phalluses, uteruses, female bodies and even embryos are imprisoned within lattices and matrices of mechanical sarcophagi from which they cannot escape, just as the human body, under the highly technicized conditions of late capitalism, has been captured by science. The appropriation of the brain by psychopharmaceuticals; the appropriation of natural birth by in vitro fertilization, animal cloning and stem cell research; the implantation of RFID chips into the skin; and the ever-tightening structural coupling between brain and video screen are all caught and perceived by Giger's art in this fabulous book.

But in *Alien*, something else is going on. The signifiers have been *removed* from the Gigerian sign regime and they have infected the industrial environment of the spaceship *Nostromo*, where they are currently running amok and overcoding that environment with their *own* sign regime. Just as the alien had burst out of Kane's chest from the inside, so too, from this scene onward, it is bursting out of the ship's industrial environment *from within*, and overcoding that environment with its own biomorphic and self-organizing signifiers, signifiers that resist capture by the industrial sign regime. The semiotics are therefore the very *opposite* of those in Giger's art book, which are uniformly images of the capture and constraining of biology by industrio-morphic technoscapes.

Just as the titans of the earth, which have been caught and captured onto the inside of a mechanical environment since the age of satellites, GPS navigation and drones, are raising havoc with record heat waves, ever-gigantifying hurricanes and enormous tsunamis, so too, in *Alien*, the biomorphic sign regime of Giger's signifiers is erupting from within *outwards*. The alien, as it rapidly and astonishingly changes forms, seems to explode across the inside of the *Nostromo*, leaving trails of slime, cast off epidermises, and dead crustacean forms in its wake. The alien will soon be creating, on one of the ship's levels—shown only in the director's cut of the film released in 2003—its own biomorphic environment, where it stores its victims and wraps them into cocoons like spiders do with their victims.

In short, sign regime A is being overcoded and completely reterritorialized by sign regime B to create a third, hybrid sign regime that will be composed of signifiers taken from both regimes. Like the semiotics of a virus, which hi-jacks the cell's nucleus to force it to make copies of the virus which then explode from within outwards (thus destroying the cell), so too, the alien always proceeds by erupting from a biological center that moves outwards towards an unknown periphery, but always with the intent of overcoding the industrial sign regime with its own semiotics. The alien, unlike the biological unfortunates of Giger's paintings, resists capture by science and technology and is always way ahead of it.

Eventually, its overcodings will have the effect of destroying the ship entirely, just as the alien first destroyed

Kane by exploding from out of his stomach.

Labyrinth
(1:08:18 – 1:14:33)

The next shot features a close-up of Parker's face explaining to the rest of the crew that whatever got Brett was a very large creature. Dallas then asks Ripley if she's certain that it took Brett away into the air shaft and she replies that it definitely disappeared with him into one of the cooling ducts. Parker then reiterates that it is using the air ducts to move around the ship.

Lambert then asks if there is any possibility that Brett could still be alive, to which Ripley gives an emphatic "no." But Dallas, studying the ship's architectural plans, suggests that the route the alien is using could work to their advantage since the air duct empties out into the main airlock. He further elaborates that there is only one big opening along the way, which could be sealed off while they then track down the creature, drive it into the airlock and zap it away into outer space.

Parker emphasizes how huge the creature has become, though, and Ash gives forth the interesting comment that it's "Kane's son." There is a pause for a moment while the crew digests that statement and then Ripley asks Ash what the science department has to say in the way of suggestions. Ash explains that the creature has adapted remarkably well to the ship's environment, but that the only thing they don't know about is how it responds to temperature. When Ripley asks him to clarify what he means, Ash points out that most animals retreat from fire, to which Dallas agrees. He then asks Parker to rig up three or four flamethrowers, and Parker says that he'll need about twenty minutes to do that. Lambert asks who gets to go into the vents, and Ripley volunteers, but Dallas vetoes that, and tells her that she and Ash will take the main airlock while Parker and Lambert will cover that maintenance opening. He, the ship's captain, is going into the vents.

In the next scene, the camera pulls back out of the main airlock, which is demarcated now as a zone that is off-limits by a twirling yellow siren as Ripley and Ash close the entrance to it. There follows a shot of Parker and Lambert sealing off the maintenance opening, which is shown dilating in a spiral fashion into an open position with an irritating sound like fingers drawn along a chalkboard.

Inside the dark and narrow air shaft now, Dallas is shown moving about with a flashlight and a flamethrower in each hand. He informs Ripley and Ash that he has arrived at the first junction. Ripley, on her headset, reassures him that she is listening. Dallas asks for a similar confirmation from Parker and Lambert who tell him through their headsets that they, too, are in position. Lambert has the motion detector device and she tells Dallas that she is working on getting a reading of his position. The camera shows a tiny electronic blue grid that maps out the air shaft and will detect any motion inside of it.

Ripley then tells Dallas that the airlock is open and ready, and Dallas confirms that he too is ready. Inside the air shaft another vent spirals shut with a scraping sound as Dallas seals it off.

A close-up shot of Lambert's motion tracking device reveals a single round dot that indicates Dallas's position, and she tells him through her headset that she now has a reading on him. Dallas is then shown crawling through the vent, flamethrower flickering in one hand, and the flashlight casting a dim vanilla light that is scarcely enough to push back the darkness inside the vent. He tells them to open the hatch to the third junction, which then spirals open before him. Only the sound of Dallas's breathing echoing through the vent can be heard, along with the ever-present, and slightly ominous beeping sound of Lambert's motion tracker that is following his position.

Dallas tells them that he has gone through the vent and orders Ripley to close all the hatches behind him. Two more vents spiral shut as Dallas moves past them, taking a turn in the tunnel ahead of him.

The sound of Lambert's voice is heard telling Dallas to halt for a moment since she believes she now has the alien on her tracking device. The tiny electronic grid on her motion detector now shows *two* blips instead of one, and the alien approaching from the *left* side of the screen on a parallel trajectory toward Dallas who is off to the right.

Dallas asks her where the alien is supposed to be located, but all she can say is that it is somewhere around the third junction. Dallas pauses in the cramped tunnel, looks behind him in the gloomy darkness, and then resolves to move forward.

Lambert tells him that her tracker readout indicates that the alien is right near him, so he's going to have to be careful. Dallas pauses at a junction, looks up and then down two different shafts, and then blasts a jet of flame through the shaft below him. He does it again for good measure, and then tells the crew that he is right at the third junction and is preparing to descend into it. He climbs down a ladder, and then Lambert is shown banging the side of her device as though it weren't working properly. Parker asks her what's wrong with the device, as now there is only *one* blip registering on its screen, and Lambert tells Dallas that he will need to hold his position for a moment, as she's lost the signal indicating the location of the creature.

He asks whether she's certain, and she tells him to look around him, that it must be there somewhere. Dallas's right hand happens at that moment to fall into a trail of slime that he picks up with his fingers and examines. As he analyzes the slime in his right hand, Dallas tells Lambert to check the monitor again, and that she might be getting some sort of interference. She tells him, her voice now obviously worried, that he needs to *look* carefully around him because the alien is right near his location.

Dallas then blasts the tunnel with his flamethrower while Lambert tells him that the creature *must* be near him. Dallas, sitting in a squatting position, now seems confused and afraid for the first time, and he asks Lambert whether he's clear to get the hell out of there.

At that moment, a *second* blip now reappears on Lambert's detector, a blip that is moving very rapidly toward Dallas's position from the left. Lambert, frantic now, tells him that the creature is now moving directly toward him. Dallas pauses, having no idea in which direction to go. Lambert yells at him to get out of the shaft and at once he hops onto the ladder nearby and begins to descend it. Unknowingly, however, he is heading directly for the creature and Lambert screams at him to go the other way. Just as he reaches the bottom of the ladder, he shines the flashlight in one direction, sees nothing, and then turns it to shine it in the other direction, fully revealing the creature which now reaches out to grab him with open arms.

No response is forthcoming when the other crewmembers inquire after him into their intercoms. The alien has taken him. He is gone.

Now, the first thing to note about this scene is that its semiotics are exactly the opposite of those of the previous sequence involving Brett's death, which took place in a very wide open space, whereas Dallas's capture (not death, exactly, as the director's cut later shows us) occurs inside of a tight, narrow and constricted series of tunnels. Ridley Scott admitted that in the wide open space of the vehicle maintenance warehouse where Brett was killed that he was going after a kind of "Gothic" feel, constructing a sort of cathedral-like space. In this sequence, however, the Gothic sense of Infinite Space that motivated the West to create the late metaphysical age imagination of perspectival space in the fifteenth century has been scrapped and traded out for a more mythical *pre*-perspectival space, the space, namely, of the labyrinth.

As the alien overcodes the *Nostromo* with its own sign regime, the sequence that involves Dallas's death has the effect of *stepping down* the sense of sight and *stepping up* the audile-tactile acoustical space that McLuhan made so famous. Unlike the rational, linear, connected corridors and spaces of the *Nostromo*—which belong to Sign Regime A, that of the late metaphysical age—the space which the alien uses to move about in the air ducts is disorienting, irrational and confusing. The alien is *undoing* the codes of the metaphysical age, which include those of perspectival space which favored the sense of sight and was built upon the discovery of Arabic optical theories during the early Renaissance, especially the theories of Al-Hazen. The retrieval of Arabian optics laid the basis for the Italian creation of perspectivally-correct space as an empty container *inside which* all objects are located and scaled to exactly the same rational proportions. This enabled mechanically-inclined geniuses like Leonardo da Vinci to imagine and draw their machines in three dimensions, which in turn laid the basis for the arrival of Cartesian phase space and all its *x, y, z* vectors for charting and creating three-dimensional machines.

The alien, as I've said, is attacking, overcoding and reterritorializing the codes of Sign Regime A, those of the scientific-industrial complex that was made possible by the discovery of visual, optically correct space in the fifteenth century. Without it, such complex machines as we have nowadays come to take for granted wouldn't even exist.

In this scene, the alien uses the *Nostromo*'s air ducts to move about, and leads Dallas on a chase in which it has the advantage, since it does not rely on the sense of sight to move about. Though the original design for the alien in Giger's *Necronom IV* painting had eyes, Ridley Scott specifically had Giger remove the eyes from the alien's crescent-shaped head in order to make it more interesting. The idea is that the alien relies upon senses *other than* those of sight, and so it moves naturally and easily about through the interiors of a labyrinth-like system of air ducts which scientists and engineers, or pragmatists like Dallas, have difficulty navigating.

The labyrinth is an extremely ancient mythological kind of space: it is directionless and deliberately disorienting, for it is not a kind of space based upon optics, but rather upon haptics.[44] Labyrinths, furthermore, were constructed—as King Minos had his engineer Daedalus do for him—to contain and hide monsters inside them, such as the shameful Minotaur, the child of an incestuous union between a human—Minos's wife Pasiphae—and an animal, a white bull sent up to Minos to sacrifice, but which he failed to perform. As Ash remarks in this scene, the alien, too, is the offspring of an incestuous union between a human—Kane—and an alien species which impregnated him with its embryo. It is the classic monster, then, inside the labyrinth which requires a special kind of hero—in Greek myth, this was Theseus—to kill it (in the present film it will be, not the traditional captain of the ship, but a woman).

The alien, in short, is reterritorializing the *Nostromo*, and transforming it into a pre-perspectival labyrinth inside which it moves about using non-visual sense organs that rely more, perhaps, upon the sense of touch—and possibly smell—than sight.[45]

The late metaphysical age that began in the fifteenth century was, above all, an optical age of imagining space full of perspectivally correct and self-sufficient entities in the mode of what Heidegger termed *Vorhandenheit*.[46] Such entities are quantitatively mapped and charted, but they are denuded from the physical qualities of a specific *Umwelt* inside which they are contained.

The creature in Ridley Scott's *Alien* is slowly undoing and scrambling all the codes of the metaphysical—a.k.a. Derrida's logocentric—age, and replacing them with ancient mythical and matriarchal codes from its own sign regime, those of Sign Regime B. It is creating a *new* cartography inside the ship, one based on older, more pre-rational vectors and codes.

The crew of the *Nostromo* are now in the process of realizing just what the creature is doing: remaking and mapping *its own* world on the *inside* of their miniaturized absolute world island that is the product of centuries of science and engineering techniques based upon replacing the codes of the mythical age. The alien, bit by bit, is scrapping *those* codes and replacing them with a new—and also very much more ancient—cartography that will cause the crew to realize that their only solution to the problem of an unbeatable creature is to abandon ship.

Ash

(1:14:34 – 1:25:57)

Parker now slams Dallas's flamethrower down on the table before the rest of the crew and tells them that he and Lambert found no trace of Dallas at all, not even any blood. When a long pause ensues, Parker becomes frustrated and asks why nobody has anything to say, to which Ripley, who is now in command, says that she is thinking. She says that unless somebody has a better idea that they will then continue on with Dallas's plan, to which Lambert replies that she must be crazy. Ripley asks her if she's got a better idea, and Lambert suggests that they just abandon ship and take their chances in the shuttle, but Ripley cuts her off and points out that the shuttle will not accommodate more than three people. Lambert then suggests that they draw straws, but Parker says he isn't going to draw any straws but that he's for killing the creature immediately.

Ripley is open to suggestions, so she offers to talk about methods of killing the alien. Parker starts cutting her off with his impatience and she has to raise her voice at him to get him to shut up and listen. She offers the plan of sealing off every vent and every bulkhead and then trapping the creature in the airlock and blowing it into outer space. She asks, with some irritation, if that is acceptable to Parker, and he says only if it means killing the creature. She says that it obviously means killing the creature. She then asks him how they're doing on weapons and Parker says they're fine other than that the flamethrower he is holding needs refueling. Ripley asks him to go and refuel it. She tells Ash, who has been listening silently, to go with him, but Parker tells him he can manage on his own and disappears.

Ash stands up and turns his back to Ripley, as though he is thinking, but Ripley, who has been annoyed with him all along, asks him whether he or Mother have any useful suggestions. Ash responds, quietly, that he is still "collating," which Ripley finds hard to believe. Ash, still with his back turned to her, asks her what she would like him to do, and Ripley tells him to continue doing exactly what he's been doing: that is to say, nothing. She says that she now has access to Mother and will get her own answers. Ash gives her a mock salute and then walks away.

The next scene shows Ripley entering the darkened corridor that leads to the inner sanctum of Mother, the ship's computer. The door slides up with a hiss, and once inside the vanilla-colored octagonal room, she seats herself at the controls and begins punching questions into the keyboard. A green electronic screen lights up, indicating that Mother is awake and ready for interface. Ripley first asks for clarification on the science division's inability to deal effectively with the alien. The computer simply replies that it cannot clarify her question. Ripley then requests further enhancement, but the computer tells her that Special Order 937 is for science officer eyes only. When she types in an emergency command override to find out the nature of the order, the computer explains to her that Special Order 937 involves rerouting the *Nostromo* to new coordinates in order to pick up and gather a life specimen and then return with it to earth. All other considerations are secondary, including the crew, which are, as Mother puts it, "expendable."

Ripley, devastated by this information, leans back in her seat to find that Ash has snuck into the module and is now presently seated beside her. He tells her, politely, that there *is* an explanation for all this, but she explodes at him, shoving him back against the wall with all her strength and telling him that she doesn't want to hear his explanations. For the first time in the film, she breaks into tears, incredulous at how the Weyland-Yutani corporation has treated them.

She hits the control to open the door, then marches out into the antechamber and presses the switch for the intercom, asking whether Parker or Lambert can hear her. She receives no reply and then turns to march down another corridor when the door slides shut in front of her. She turns around to find Ash standing ominously silent behind her and she orders him to open the door, now becoming frightened by his demeanor.

She tries another corridor, but Ash closes off that escape route, too, by overriding the controls that open and close the door. Ripley, both frightened and angry simultaneously, now approaches Ash, adrenalin running through her body as he stands there, looking quietly at her, while beads of a milky fluid leak like sweat down the side of his face. When she tries to get past him, he sticks his right arm out, blocking her way, then reaches with his left hand and grabs a clump of her hair which he pulls from her head as she attempts to dash away from his reach, crawling upon the floor on all fours like an animal. He pursues, however, grabbing her by the back of her jumpsuit and smashing her with great force into the wall. He pauses a moment, then picks her up again and tosses her, with enormous strength, into an alcove, where she lies flat on her back, momentarily unconscious.

The alcove is covered with pornographic pictures clipped from magazines and pasted to its walls in collage fashion. There are also little kitschy objects dangling from wires that echo the chains dangling from the warehouse ceiling in the scene which had involved Brett's death. Ash picks up a pornographic magazine, rolls it up into a cylinder, and in an act that echoes the face-hugger sliding its phallus down Kane's throat, tries to shove the cylindrical magazine down Ripley's throat in order to choke her to death. She immediately awakens and begins choking, while at just that moment Parker and Lambert arrive and Parker asks Ash what the fuck he thinks he's doing. Lambert attempts to grab him from behind to pull him away, while Parker tries to wrestle the magazine out of Ripley's mouth, to which Ash responds by reaching with a clawed left hand to grab Parker's right chest and squeeze the life out of it. Parker falls to the ground in agony, but then immediately springs back up, pushes Lambert out of the way, and grabs a metal canister which he uses to smash into the side of Ash's head. The effect of the blow on Ash is catastrophic: it causes him to go spinning and twisting wildly out of control like a human top, spewing milk-white fluid from his mouth as he does so.

Parker then hits his head again with the metal canister, and to everyone's surprise, Ash's head simply comes off and falls backward, where it dangles by a thread from his neck. Parker continues beating Ash with the canister until Ash falls to the ground, spewing forth milky fluids while Parker announces that "Ash is a goddamned robot!"

But Ash still has some fight left in him and he leaps, head dangling, at Parker, knocking him to the ground in another attempt at a homicidal assault. Parker yells for Lambert to help him and she reaches for one of the cattle prods, jabbing it into the open circuitry of Ash's neck, which electrocutes him and causes him to seize up.

In the next scene, Ash's body, with various organic-looking circuits and fiber optic wires leaking out of his open neck, is lying on a table, with his head set beside the body. Parker's voice can be heard asking why the company sent them a robot, and while Ripley rewires Ash's head, she tells Parker that all she can think of is that they must have wanted the alien for their weapons division. Ripley tells Parker to plug Ash back in, and when he protests, she explains that he may know how to kill the alien.

Ripley picks up some sort of electrical instrument, which she then applies beneath Ash's head on the inside of his skull, causing sparks to bring him back to life in a scene that echoes Michelangelo's transmission of the spark of life to Adam on the Sistine Ceiling (except that this time the spark is transmitted by a woman). Ripley sets Ash's head up so that it is stable and then asks Ash if he can hear her. When there is no response, she yells his name and bangs on the table, which brings his eyes popping open and as he struggles to speak, spews forth more milk-white fluid that dribbles down his chin. "Yes," he says, his voice now sounding electronified, "I can hear you."

Ripley then asks him what his special order was, to which Ash replies that she read it and that he thought it was clear. But Ripley wants to hear him say it, and so she demands that he repeat it. He tells her that the order was to bring back the alien life form, priority number one, all other priorities rescinded. Parker, infuriated, stands up and asks what the company intended to do with their lives. Ash, calm as ever, repeats that all other priorities are rescinded.

Ripley then demands to know how they can kill the alien, but Ash tells her that they can't. Ash explains to them that they still don't understand that they are dealing with a *perfect* organism, an organism whose structural perfection is matched only by its hostility. Lambert tells him, disgustedly, that he admires it, but Ash clarifies that he admires its *purity* and that it is a survivor unclouded by delusions of conscience or morality.

Parker tells Ripley that he's heard enough and asks her to pull the plug. When she reaches for it, Ash tells her to wait just one more moment. He then says to them that he can't lie to them about their chances but that they have his sympathies. And then he smiles.

Ripley now pulls the plug that deactivates Ash and tells Parker that the plan is now to blow up the ship and take their chances in the shuttle. Parker stands up and grabs Lambert's arm to get her moving ahead of him. As the two women move through the corridor, Parker pauses at the threshold and then turns back and roasts Ash with his flamethrower.

This entire sequence is a turning point in the film, for it involves a structural transformation in the character of Ripley, who now, as a signifier, is transferred from Sign Regime A to that of Sign Regime B. Whereas in Sign Regime A, she had merely functioned as a warrant officer aboard a mining vessel, in Sign Regime B, she has been recoded as an Amazonian warrior.

In J.J. Bachofen's schema—who unearthed the epoch of "Mother Right" in his famous 1861 book of the same name—the historical phase of matriarchy was inaugurated by the formation of the Amazons who gathered together in reaction to sexual abuses inflicted upon them by men. The earliest epoch of human history for Bachofen wasn't matriarchal, but an age which he called "Aphroditic-hetaeric," meaning an age of sexual promiscuity between men and women when people lived in tribes and bands and were never certain of whose offspring belonged to which father. (That resemblances between children and their parents would most likely not have gone unnoticed seems to have escaped Bachofen).[47]

The formation of the Amazons, however, inaugurated the second historical epoch, that of the "Demetrian-matriarchic," in which agriculture was invented, along with the institution of marriage, and children took the names of their mothers, not their fathers. Bachofen's evidence for the existence of this age was mostly linguistic and mythological, but there are suggestions that at Neolithic sites like Catalhoyuk, women were held in higher esteem than men, since their graves were much more richly furnished with trinkets and jewelry than those of the men. Statues of goddesses, furthermore, predominate at that site, as they do at many other Neolithic sites from around 8000 BC or so. And we know that some vestiges of these matrilineal times survived clear down into ancient Egypt, since the pharaoh on the throne had to be able to claim rightful descent from his mother's side of the family, not his father's.

But Bachofen says that the epoch of the Demetrian-matriarchal was bounded at both ends by reactionary rebellions of the Amazons who, at the climax of the age of the Mothers, represented a *degeneration* of matriarchy (since they spurned the institution of marriage), along with the Dionysus cults, which were mostly composed of female worshippers and which represented a regression back to the sexual promiscuity of the original Aphroditic-hetaeric epoch. All the various wars against the Amazons in Greek mythology which occur at about the time of the Trojan War, or just slightly before it—wars in which Achilles defeats Penthesilea on the battlefield, or in which Heracles steals the girdle of the Amazon queen Hippolyta (Theseus and Bellerophon engaged in wars against the Amazons, too)--

all these wars signified the onset of the age of patriarchy, which Bachofen designated as the "Apollonian-rational," from about 1200 BC forward. Bachofen, furthermore, underscored the fact that most of the wars later fought by the Romans were not fought for mere economic interests, but conquests of peoples, such as the Carthaginians or the Sabines, who primarily worshipped goddesses. (Bachofen's influence on Nietzsche's use of the terms Dionysian and Apollonian, in his 1872 treatise on aesthetics known as *The Birth of Tragedy*, should be quite evident here).

In my book *Rage and the Word: Gilgamesh, Akhenaten, Moses and the Birth of the Metaphysical Age*,[48] I designated the date of approximately 1200 BC as demarcating the period of the collapse of the first generation of high civilization—that, namely, of the Mesopotamians and the Egyptians—and the rise of the second generation with the Greeks and the Jews, neither of whom were much concerned with the afterlife, as Franz Borkenau has pointed out in his book *End and Beginning*, building on Toynbee's theories regarding three distinct generations of high civilization.[49] For Borkenau, Homer and Moses signified the rise of the so-called "death accepting" cultures which had little interest in funerary cults—which are already in disintegration, as Nietzsche's friend Erwin Rohde pointed out in his 1893 book *Psyche*, by the time of the *Iliad*[50]—by contrast with the previous epoch of the "death transcending" cultures of Mesopotamia and Egypt, both of which were obsessed with the survival of the soul in the afterlife. With the onset of the Greeks and the Jews, however (according to Borkenau) the realm of the dead grew dark and (according to Bachofen) patriarchy began to set in and children began taking their father's names. All this, for Bachofen, is signified by the victories of Perseus, Theseus et.al. in their wars against the Amazons, who represent for him the last dying gasp of the matriarchal epoch.

Now, just as in the previous scene in *Alien* of Dallas's death in the air shafts, the myth of Zeus's victory over the Titan child of Gaia named Typhon—who was human from the waist up and serpent from the waist down—was replayed in *reverse*, with Typhon *winning* this time by gobbling up the ship's captain (and therefore its Zeus equivalent), so in the struggle between Ripley and Ash, the wars of the patriarchal heroes against the Amazons is *re*-fought, with the victory going this time to the Amazons.

Ash is Father Science incarnate. As an android that mimics human life perfectly, he is the ultimate achievement of Sign Regime A, its greatest creation and the only entity that it has to offer to stand beside the alien as a creature of perfection. Ash has been cooked up in a laboratory somewhere and so given birth to by means of the metaphysical vulva which Father Science has appropriated from the Mothers, and he is therefore a sort of equivalent signifier—a metonymic part for the whole, in other words—of the metaphysical age of Sign Regime A, which has been busy replacing the natural morphogenetic powers of the Mothers with artificial substitutes.

But Ash, great achievement though he is, pales by comparison to the alien, which metamorphoses so rapidly that one can barely keep up with the various phases of its transformations. It is indeed a Titan that has crawled forth from the underworld of such creatures repressed by the building up of the metaphysical age which has deprivileged them by assigning to them a negative valency and thrusting them down into the civilizational underworld. If Ash is artificial life made complete and perfect, then the alien is the child of the Mothers, an entity which supremely embodies the processes of self-organization and morphogenesis that

Father Science envies and tries to imitate in his petri dishes but cannot *quite* match.

Ripley's victory over Ash in this scene—admittedly, with help from Parker and Lambert, though it is she who is now in charge—is a replay of the heroic wars of the Greek patriarchal heroes against the Amazons *in reverse*. It is the Amazons who are on the rise now, and so there is a secret metaphysical connection between Ripley-as-Amazon and the alien, which is a signifier left over from the time of Zeus's wars against the Titans and the Giants in Hesiod's *Theogony*.

Ash is right about one thing: the alien *cannot* be destroyed, captured or encompassed by the artificial life technologies of Weyland-Yutani (think of Wieland the smith in German mythology). Instead, it requires being outsmarted by a more developed and intelligent signifier that is part of its *own* sign regime, albeit a signifier—Ripley in this case—who, unbeknownst to herself, is crossing over from one sign regime to the next, and in the process helping to construct Sign Regime C, which as I've said, is a sort of hybrid product of the crossing of signifiers back and forth between the two regimes which is mapped out by the thematic cartography of *Alien*.

Parker and Lambert
(1:27:58 – 1:32:39)

Ripley, Parker and Lambert are now shown walking down one of the ship's narrow corridors. Ripley asks Parker how much time they would have after they program the ship to self-destruct and Parker tells her that they will have only ten minutes from that point onward. Ripley says that they will then need supplies of coolant for the shuttle's air support system. The three arrive at a junction of corridors and pause a moment, watchful of the alien, and then Ripley tells Parker and Lambert to go down to C level and get the necessary coolant canisters while she gets the ship ready for auto-destruct. She says that they will meet back up at this spot in seven minutes and then blow the creature out into space as the ship destroys itself. Parker agrees and tells Ripley to take care of herself while he and Lambert descend down a ladder to C deck.

Ripley now makes for the bridge, where she punches the controls to release the shuttle from its bay. Pinning her hair up, she is then about to start programming the ship's auto-destruct system when she hears the cry of her cat, Jones. (Ripley's cat companion, by the way, marks her descent as a signifier from the ancient cat goddess who is always accompanied by a lion, from Inanna in ancient Sumer, through Shiva's consort Parvati [whose *vahana* was a tiger] down to Cybele in Palestine, whose chariot was pulled by a pair of lions [shown below]).

The scene then cuts to C deck, inside the same vast Gothic space in which Brett was killed, where Parker and Lambert are now pushing a dolly and lighting their way with a flashlight. They roll past several sets of enormous copper-ringed pillars and then arrive at the bay where the canisters are kept. Parker covers Lambert with the flamethrower while she begins frantically pulling canisters out of their storage compartments and loading them onto the dolly.

The scene then cuts back to a shot of Ripley arriving on an upper deck via a white ladder. She retrieves the cat carrier from a white storage cabinet that is full of spacesuits and makes her way back to the bridge.

Down below on C deck, meanwhile, Parker and Lambert have stuffed their dolly full of supplies and begun pushing it back in the other direction. They reach another storage room, where Parker tells Lambert to "check the bottles."

They begin frantically loading more canisters.

The scene cuts again back to Ripley, who has made her way to the bridge, where she searches for the cat amongst the cramped consoles and pilot seats. The cat jumps out from behind one of the seats and scares her, then darts around the corner, playing the same game it had played earlier with Brett. Ripley, startled, takes a moment to catch her breath and then walks around the front of the bridge to grab the cat and stuff him inside his cage.

On C deck, however, Lambert has now spotted the alien and is frozen with fear. A round circle of light, like a spotlight, falls upon her, which immediately fills up with the alien's shadow as it approaches her. Parker, from the other end of the room, has now seen the creature and he tells Lambert to "get out of the way" so that he can blast it with his flamethrower.

On the bridge, Ripley hears the altercation via the intercom, as Parker's voice comes over it, yelling at Lambert to get out of the way.

Back on C deck, the alien is shown with its huge crescent-shaped head unfolding itself before Lambert and rising to a standing position like a man. When Parker attempts to run at it, the alien abruptly turns and strikes him down with its long, vertebral-segmented whiplash of a tail. It then grabs him by the neck and pins him down while it opens its drooling jaws and prepares to strike him with its deadly tongue.

Ripley, meanwhile, is on the way, running at full speed down to C deck.

The alien, however, crushes Parker's skull with its toothed-tongue, and then turns its attentions back on Lambert, who is still frozen with fear and cannot move. The alien's prehensile tail, with a sharp spike on the tip of it, slides in between her feet and goes up her back, where it punctures a hole into her spinal column. The ship fills with her screams.

By the time Ripley arrives on the scene, it is too late: Parker is lying dead on the floor, blood dripping from the half of his skull that has been cracked open, and Lambert's bare feet—oddly—are shown dangling with streams of blood dripping down them, as though the creature has pinned her up on the wall somewhere.

Ripley turns and flees.

In this sequence, note that the alien has specifically killed the ship's navigator, Lambert, as well as its last surviving mechanic, Parker. It has, in other words, rendered the *Nostromo* completely inert: directionless in space, and without someone who could fix its ruptured mechanical systems, it has now become the very ghost ship that the opening image at the film's beginning suggested that it might be.

In the lore of the ancients, there was a belief that a certain type of fish known as a remora (which means "delay" in Latin) would magnetically attach itself to the underside of a boat and stop the boat dead in its tracks with a magical power. Pliny the Elder believed that such a fish attached itself to Mark Antony's boat during the Battle of Actium and caused him to lose the battle. The alien, in this sequence, essentially corresponds to the magical remora fish that halts ships dead in their tracks, even a gigantic miracle of engineering such as the *Nostomo*. The creature has now completely seized control of the ship and rendered it inutile.

Even if Ripley could kill the alien at this point, she would most likely be unable to pilot the craft by herself. It has now become an absolute world island that has been punctured, ruptured and rendered uninhabitable for humans.

Ripley, as I've pointed out, has been transferred from one sign regime to another: from Sign Regime A, where she functioned as the ship's warrant officer, she has now been transferred to Sign Regime B, where she functions as an Amazonian warrior. However, the fact that she is essentially a hybrid signifier of signs taken from both regimes indicates that she actually belongs to a *third* regime that the alien is in the process of creating, as it overcodes and reterritorializes the *Nostromo*.

Indeed, the micro-world of the *Nostromo* has now been lost irretrievably, and habitability has contracted to the confines of its shuttle, a tiny lifeboat that will be sent forth from a sinking mechanical island—a sort of outer space equivalent of a *Deepwater Horizon*-type drilling platform-- that has been rendered useless by a *single* biohazardous being.

In a way, the alien's crushing of Parker's skull and drilling its tail into Lambert's spinal cord—thereby disrupting the functioning of her central nervous system—is analogous to the destruction of the ship's brain and nervous system. There is only Mother, the ship's uterine computer and central electronic nervous system remaining, but she can now no longer perform her maternal functions of running an artificial substitute for a natural, Gaian environment. The only role left for Mother to play now is that of a sort Kali figure of black death and destruction.

Robbed of her capacity to watch over her entities, Mother must now be recoded to devour the world island that she was created to protect.

Underworld
(1:32:40 – 1:36:14)

Ripley now begins running through corridors with spinning yellow hazard lights as she makes her way back to the bridge in order to program the ship for auto-destruction. She pulls down a silver bar that causes a catch to release the lid of the emergency destruct system. After quickly reading the instructions, she presses a sequence of white buttons that release four large bolts, then begins to screw each of the bolts into its correct socket. The voice of the ship's computer, Mother, now gives off a warning alarm and informs the ship that there is danger and that it will destroy itself in T-minus ten minutes. The ship's video monitors fill with blinking red and blue crosses and countdowns on them. Mother then announces that the option to override the auto-destruct will expire in T minus five minutes.

In the 2003 director's cut of the film, a scene has been put back in place by Ridley Scott, who originally cut it because he thought it slowed the film down at this point. The scene begins with Ripley running along a corridor that is filled with blasting steam vents and then she descends down a ladder, flamethrower in hand, to a darkened storage room not yet seen in the film (it could, however, be located on C deck). The only illumination comes from the flickering light of the flamethrower, which transforms the room into a sort of miniature cavern. In the shaky darkness, she discovers that part of the wall has been covered by the alien with a kind of hive that has a texture to it reminiscent of the interior of the derelict spacecraft where they found the eggs. Then, to her horror, she turns and sees Dallas, who is still alive, although only barely. The alien has created a cocoon around his body and somehow affixed him to the wall. Brett, too, has been cocooned further up on the wall above Dallas, where he is almost completely covered by a leathery sack.

Dallas's voice can barely be heard as he begs Ripley to kill him. Ripley hesitates only for a moment, but then steps back and torches the alien's entire lair, killing Dallas and burning Brett to cinders.

Notice that in this scene, the alien is beginning to *fold up* the inside of the derelict spacecraft and to place it on the inside of the *Nostromo*. In hybridizing the two sign regimes, the alien is overcoding and replacing the semiotics of Sign Regime A with those of Sign Regime B to create a third sign regime that is composed of signifiers from both of them.

Ripley stops this overcoding process dead in its tracks by torching this center-to-periphery explosion of alien semiotics from within outwards. The alien's overcoding of the ship from within corresponds to its reterritorializing of Kane's body as that of a pregnant female. The movement of the creature's strategy is always from a center that begins somewhere on the inside of Sign Regime A and then explodes outwards in all directions, covering the interior of the *Nostromo* in alien signifiers.

Note furthermore that the alien is in the process of creating *its own* Underworld, down into which it is now repressing signifier equivalents from the metaphysical age of Zeus (Dallas) and Hephaestus (the blacksmith). It is thereby *reversing* the process in which Zeus's reign was dependent upon his thrusting of the Titans and giants down into the underworld of Tartaros (shown below). The alien now is creating an underworld in which it counters this ancient process by thrusting signifiers from Sign Regime A down into the depths below, while *its own* signifiers are on the rise.

The only way to stop this explosion from within is by destroying the world island of the *Nostromo* itself, so that it cannot be reterritorialized and transformed into the interior of the derelict spacecraft.

Auto-Destruct
(1:36:15 – 1:43:27)

In the next scene, Ripley is shown emerging from below decks, her face cautiously peering out from the well of the ladder for signs of alien presence. When the coast appears to be clear, she comes out of the well and grabs the cat carrier with Jones inside of it. Alarms are going off all over the ship, with yellow sirens highlighting the danger. As Mother's voice comes over the intercom, she informs the ship that the option to override the auto-destruct expires in three minutes. Ripley, approaching the corridor that leads to the shuttle, stands against the wall in a blinking strobe light while she glances round the corner and catches sight of the alien just as it is standing up.

Terrified now, she slinks down the wall and rounds the corner going back down the corridor that leads to the bridge, just as the jaws of the creature appear around the corner. The alien pauses for a moment, seeming to consider the cat inside his cage, then knocks the cage aside.

As Ripley frantically runs back toward the bridge, Mother's voice announces that the option to expire the override terminates in T minus one minute. As Mother begins the countdown from 30, Ripley hurriedly tries to reverse the ship's auto-destruct programming. But it is now too late. By the time Ripley has turned the cooling unit back on, Mother has announced that the option to override has now expired. Another siren goes off as Mother explains that the ship will automatically self-destruct in T minus five minutes. Infuriated, Ripley calls her a bitch and smashes one of her video monitors with the butt end of her flamethrower.

Having no choice now, Ripley races back down the corridor leading to the shuttle, in hopes that the alien is no longer blocking the passage. When she cautiously arrives at the entry, there is, fortunately, no sign of the alien, and she appears to be in luck. Grabbing the cat cage with Jones inside, Ripley very carefully makes her way through the airlock and into the shuttle, while flames leap from the ship's corridors behind her. She punches the button to seal off the hatch, then seats herself in the pilot's chair and begins frantically hitting switches to launch the shuttle as Mother's voice announces that she has one minute to abandon ship.

The shuttle's bay unlocks, and Ripley straps herself in as the shuttle is lowered from the mother ship into launch position. Mother begins another 30 second countdown as the shuttle is launched and races away from the ship at top speed, while Ripley, sweating and anxious, hangs on. At the ten second mark, she watches as the *Nostromo* recedes off into the distance behind her, then explodes in a rainbow flurry of colors that remind one of the exploding Death Star at the conclusion of *Star Wars*.

Under her breath, Ripley then mutters, "I got you, you son of a bitch."

The overall impression of this sequence is a classic scenario of what historian Arnold J. Toynbee referred to as "the loss of command over an environment."[51] This is a situation that occurs in the late phases of civilizations when their entropy content is increasing and the civilization's overall ability to control its environment gradually weakens. It happens to them all, eventually: in Mesopotamia the gradual salinization of the soils ruined that society's ability to self-organize; deforestation in ancient Greece, due to shipbuilding, put economic pressures on that society that led to fratricidal warfare; and today, industrial civilization is slowly roasting the planet alive, causing sea-level rise, ever higher ocean temperatures and record-breaking hurricanes.

The industrially organized spaceship *Nostromo* suffers a similar fate: in this case, the incursion of a biohazard inside of a carefully controlled and maintained environment that eventually causes that environment to spiral into unmanageability. It is a bit like Baudrillard's theory of evil in his book *The Transparency of Evil*, in which he there defines evil in contemporary society as that which disrupts the smooth functioning of any system. Thus, AIDS disrupts the smooth functioning of the immune system, just as terrorism disrupts the ability of the state apparatus to function normally, while peaks and troughs in the global economic flow causes perturbations that disrupt the economy.[52]

The alien in Ridley Scott's film is a perfect analogue to Baudrillard's "evil," which is not really evil from any morally considered standpoint, but rather from a functional standpoint, since the creature disrupts the ship's ability to function by overcoding it with its own sign regime. Evil, for Baudrillard, is that which must be expelled from the system in order for the system to run normally.

But the build-up of noise within systems is gradual and inevitable with all systems over time. The *Nostromo* has ceased to function as a world-island for anthropogenic survival, and serves as a perfect model for the current disruptions of the industrial civilization that has surrounded and engulfed the planet so that it is now on the inside of a highly technicized environment, an environment furthermore, which is slowly being eroded by the "evils" of monster hurricanes, tsunamis, nuclear reactor meltdowns and record heat waves. Droughts, raging wild fires and massive swarms of tornadoes have now become the "evils" on the inside of a technical civilization that is becoming increasingly difficult to master.

The Real, for Lacan, is that which cannot be assimilated into one's symbolic order, and usually amounts to the impact of a trauma. The alien in Scott's film is also the Lacanian Real that resists all assimilation into the prevailing sign regime, and instead, breaks it to pieces, so that a new one has to be formed.

Final Battle
(1:43:28 – 1:53:06)

Ripley, thinking that her maximal stress situation is over, now relaxes in her seat for a moment before standing up and retrieving her cat from the cat carrier. She places the cat inside of one of the cryo-sleep chambers and then begins to undress in preparation for her own descent into cryo-sleep. She strips down to her undershirt and white panties, and while she is in the middle of a process of flipping switches and checking dials, the alien's six-fingered hand suddenly pops from out of the mechanical circuitry of the ship's wall where it had cleverly disguised its crescent-shaped head amongst a series of similarly-shaped crescent-like units.

Ripley stifles a scream and then immediately backs into a storage closet and closes the door. Inside the closet, there are spacesuits, which gives her an idea as she watches the alien through the glass—which appears now only to want to go into some sort of hibernation. The camera, in a low angle shot, frames her lifting one leg as she steps back into the spacesuit behind her, giving the viewer a clear shot of her crotch, although it is covered in white panties. The shot is not gratuitous, however, for it reveals the film's central hidden signifier which has been at issue all along: the power struggle between the two sign regimes over the metaphysical vulva. That is to say, which regime has the right to create life: Sign Regime A, a holdover from the metaphysical age in which the Father has appropriated the paternal womb to create living forms in laboratories; or Sign Regime B, in which the creatures of Mother Earth retain the right to self-organize and metamorphose through "natural" as opposed to artificial stages. The shot of Ripley's crotch is an instance of the vulva on the register of the Real, whereas the metaphysical vulva—both on the imaginary and symbolic levels—has been implicit throughout the film as its hidden signifier.

Ripley continues to dress herself in the spacesuit, fixing the helmet in place, and once she has put on this artificial environment, she grabs and loads a harpoon gun, evoking the myth of the hunt for the great beast which had been the central concern of Melville's *Moby Dick*. Harpoons were used to kill whales in that novel—although not the white whale, which survived—and the harpoon here has a similar significance, unpacking and unfolding the history of mythological monster slayings.

Ripley, seeing that the alien is trying to sleep—its tongue stretches forth and yawns—takes a risk and steps out of the storage closet and sits down on the main control seat, where she straps herself in and then begins nervously punching buttons which release vents of steam near the alien, until she finds the precise one that awakens the creature and causes him to spill forth from his bay. Now irritated with her, the creature approaches her and she turns just in time to see its tongue getting ready to strike at her when she punches the button to open the ship's front door, which instantly depressurizes the cabin and sucks the creature out. However, it grabs onto the sides of the door frame on its way out, and so Ripley shoots it with her harpoon gun, which causes it to let go and drift into outer space. But she has closed the door too soon and the gun, still attached to the alien by means of the wire connecting it to the harpoon, gets stuck beneath it.

An exterior shot shows the alien trying to make its way back inside the ship through the engine exhaust port, but Ripley finishes it off by starting up the engines which then blast it with fire, finally killing it once and for all.

In the film's penultimate scene, Ripley is then shown seated with her cat, relaxed finally, as she speaks into the ship's data recorder all the names of the crewmembers who have been killed, along with the destruction of the *Nostromo* itself.

The final scene shows her asleep inside of her cryochamber, at peace at last and looking like some Sleeping Beauty inside of her glass coffin awaiting a suitor to awaken her with a kiss.

This final sequence functions as a sort of coda to the film's metaphysical struggle between the two sign regimes over the metaphysical vulva. Ripley, who has been transferred from Sign Regime A to Sign Regime B, and there recoded as an Amazon warrior, now becomes officially a dragon-slayer in the tradition of the great metaphysical age sign regime that was inaugurated with the Indo-Aryan and Semite invasions around 1500 BC. All the texts that eventually issued from those invasions by 1200 BC—once the dust had settled down—feature dragon-slayer myths in which a male hero—Indra in the case of the *Rig Veda*, Yahweh in the case of the Book of Genesis—take over all the signifiers from the mythical consciousness structure that had governed the first generation of civilization with the Egyptians and the Mesopotamians. Yahweh tames the waters of the abyss, called "*tehom*" after the monster Tiamat from the older Babylonian creation epic known as the *Enuma Elish*; and later on, when

Hesiod gets around to writing his *Theogony* circa 650 BC—although the myths that he preserves are from a much older period, older even than those of Homer—he describes the war of Zeus against the Titans and the Giants who are the parthenogenetically produced offspring of Gaia, the Earth Mother herself who later appears in a reduced role as Erda in the *Poetic Eddas*.

These dragon-slayer myths laid down like a layer of sediment during the metaphysical age on top of the previous mythical age all created the foundations for the rise of patriarchy and its victory over Mother Earth that eventually culminated in the Renaissance rediscovery of the texts of the Greeks—such as the writings of Euclid, Galen, Ptolemy and Plato—which inspired the late period of the metaphysical age (also known as the perspectival age) with the rise of science and the "forgetting of Being," as Heidegger called it. Being came to be understood as entities mapped into a Cartesian grid system that had the effect of deworlding them and making them "objective" and quantifiable, thus laying the foundations for the rise of the Machine Age which followed and whose tail end we are living in today. Being became understood during this epoch as a realm of transcendental subjects beholding pure objects denuded of "qualities"—mostly such secondary qualities as gave them the sensory qualities of "being in a world," such as taste, touch, smell, color, etc.

But it is during this period which Jean Gebser labeled that of the mental consciousness structure—and which Heidegger termed the metaphysical age (late phase)—that science took possession of the metaphysical vulva. Mary Shelley, writing her novel *Frankenstein* in 1818, already knew what was happening and created—at about the same time as Goethe was writing his *Faust*, which told of the same myth—one of the first myths about patriarchal science stealing the power to give birth to biological forms from the Mother and producing them artificially in laboratories.

These are actually themes explored more fully by Ridley Scott in his next film *Blade Runner*, but suffice it to say that *Alien* is not very optimistic about the ability of Father Science to replicate and to control biogenesis artificially. It presents an organism that is too smart to be caught, captured and overcoded by this sign regime (A), and instead shows the victory of this creature over that sign regime.

The creature, in the post-metaphysical age, now requires slaying by an Amazon, not a male dragon-slayer, representing the victory of the vulva over the phallus (as has been stated almost to the point of cliché, there is something "phallic" about the alien, its head, its tongue, etc.).

Ripley, so far as I know, is the first female dragon-slayer in the history of cinema, although certainly not in the history of myth, where she has put in sporadic appearances (i.e. Durga in Indian myth; or the female bodhisattva known as Kuan-yin in Chinese myth, or Tokoyo in Japanese myth).

Once her status as an anthropological type is retrieved by Scott's film, the female dragon slayer has appeared in film after film with ever increasing frequency since 1979 (even Princess Leia strangles Jabba the Hut to death in the 1983 film *Return of the Jedi*).

Currently her status as an anthropological type, however, has decayed to the level of a cliché—Quentin Tarantino's *Kill Bill*, where he has borrowed the female samurai from the graphic novels of Frank Miller, simply exhausts one by its overkill—and requires scrapping and rethinking. Cliches, as Marshall McLuhan demonstrated, have to be scrapped when they are entropically exhausted and placed onto the middenheap, from whence they are hybridized with old, discarded signifiers to become new archetypes which then give rise to new cultural forms.

Undoubtedly, this very process is taking place right now somewhere deep within the abysses of our civilizational unconscious.

But Ripley was there first.

Appendix I:
On the Sign Regimes in *Alien*

The concept of "sign regimes" is developed by Deleuze and Guattari in their book *A Thousand Plateaus*, in the chapter entitled "On Several Regimes of Signs." In that chapter, they make a distinction between five sign regimes: the *presignifying*, or tribal, sign regime; the *signifying* (or despotic) sign regime that comes into being with the rise of high civilization; the *countersignifying* regime that is always constellated by the nomadic war machine that is ever lurking on the peripheries of these civilizations; and the *postsignifying* sign regime that begins with the Hebrew rejection of the first generation of civilization in Egypt and Mesopotamia and develops the idea of subjective consciousness beginning with the figure of Moses; and then finally, an *asignifying* sign regime in which all semiotic machines are destroyed and undone on what D&G call the "plane of consistency," which is opposed to the "plane of organization" (or law) upon which the other sign regimes are always organized. But no sign regime, as they are careful to put it, is ever pure, for they are always mixed and signifiers from one regime survive into subsequent regimes and mix or hybridize with them.

For my reading of *Alien*, I have borrowed this concept and structured the film as a dichotomy of two opposed sign regimes, the structures of which are as follows:

Sign Regime A:

Signifiers are industrial, mechanical, electronic and scientific; Father Science as master signifier of entire regime; paternal womb and metaphysical vulva are primary means, initially, of giving birth to machines, and then later to artificial (biological) life, such as cloning, stem cell creation and in vitro fertilization; right-angled thinking is central to this regime and space is thought of as a container inside which all objects are scaled to the same dimensions so that they can be mapped onto the Cartesian grid; this is the age of what Derrida calls "logocentrism," in which certain signifiers are privileged over others (such as the voice over writing; or original *archai* over the copy, etc.) This sign regime also corresponds to Heidegger's metaphysical age and Jean Gebser's mental consciousness structure, which is logical, rational and syllogistic in its thought structures. Ash as opposed to the alien; the *Nostromo* as opposed to the derelict ship; the cryo-sleep pods as opposed to the alien eggs, etc. All biological and natural structures, in other words, have mechanized correlates. The bird is its prime signifier.

Sign Regime B:

This sign regime, which I have also termed "Gigerian," after the Swiss artist H.R. Giger, who did the alien designs for the film, is non-rational, mythic, curvilinear and serpentine, both in the structure of its thinking and in the way that space is organized "acoustically," as McLuhan put it; it is pre-perspectival and pre-patriarchal and primarily based upon an imaginary of mythic forms and a bestiary of zodiacal beasts;

it favors caverns and labyrinths and it is vagina-centric, rather than phallocentric, since most of its power rests upon the creativity of the earth mother herself. The Great Goddess is the master signifier here, together with her male serpent consort, who is most often depicted as her lover. The world is not open, but closed inside a uteromorphic container the boundaries of which are often depicted as a gigantic serpent such as Okeanos in Greek myth or Ananta in Indian myth, thus transforming the endless blue oceans into a sort of primal amniotic fluid. The power for the creation of forms is inside the earth itself and does not require intervention by a priest or a scientist. The primary power shaper is the shaman. Giger's derelict ship is opposed to Ron Cobb's *Nostromo*, which is basically a floating laboratory and mining platform.

Sign Regime C:

This sign regime is tricky because it is never fully formed by the conclusion of *Alien*, but only hinted at as a possibility. It is the result of a hybridizing of the previous two sign regimes by swapping signifiers and moving them around to trade places. Thus, Ripley as the ship's warrant officer in the first sign regime, is transferred to the order of Sign Regime B about halfway through the film when she takes command of the ship after Dallas's death. Kane gives birth to a creature, as in the appropriation of the imaginal vulva during the metaphysical age into a symbolic vulva, but what he gives birth to is a *naga* rather than a rational creation like Athena or a human being like Eve or a god like Christ. The alien creates its own Underworld in which it attempts to repress the signifiers of Sign Regime A, but Ripley, as an Amazon with a flamethrower instead of a spear, destroys it, just as she kills the creature itself. This sign regime, in other words, remains at the level of mere possibility, rather than actuality, and seems to hint at the creation of a regime in which both Father Science and Mother Earth cooperate to produce new forms that are half self-organizing and half-technicized.

Appendix 2:
Comparative Table of World Ages

There is a lot of discussion in this book regarding various stages, phases and epochs of world history, and I thought it might be nice for the reader to have a chart that compares the various models of history which I have drawn from in my analysis. The grand metanarrative may (or, as Peter Sloterdijk asserts, may not) be dead, but it can still be used as a hermeneutic tool to make sense out of the origins of signifiers, which always *come from somewhere*. They have usually been dislodged from the various strata of their respective world ages. Here are the main models I have used in this book:

J.J. Bachofen:

In his work, *Mother Right* (1861), Bachofen made a distinction between several epochs of world history as follows:

The Aphroditic-hetaeric epoch: a tribal age in which sexual promiscuity prevailed, marriage did not exist, and no one knew whose children belonged to whom.

The Amazonian Interlude: the Amazons then first form as a reaction against sexual abuses inflicted upon them by the men.

The Demetrian-matriarchal epoch: during the agricultural phase, marriage is invented and children take their mother's names.

Second Amazonian Interlude: the Amazons rise again, but this time they represent a degeneration of the matriarchal epoch, since they spurn the institution of marriage. They have to be conquered by patriarchal heroes like Perseus, Heracles, Bellerophon and Achilles in order to make way for the next epoch, which is patriarchal.

The Apollonian-rational: best exemplified for Bachofen by the Romans and their invention of a legal system that is rationally structured. Children now take the names of their fathers.

Jean Gebser:

In his book *The Ever-Present Origin*, Gebser divides the phases of history as follows:

The Archaic Consciousness Structure: goes way, way back into anthropoid history and cannot really be discerned, since it is lost in the mists of time.

The Magical Consciousness Structure: pertains to tribal man, and the vision of magical effects being manipulated by shamans using world lines of invisible etheric energy that connect, and unify, the world into a kind of web or cavern.

The Mythical Consciousness Structure: configures itself with the rise of high civilization, or with the Neolithic matriarchy during the agricultural epoch that precedes it (and hence would correspond to Bachofen's epoch of Mother Right). Everything is polarized in this structure: heaven vs. earth; the breath soul vs. the world soul; yin vs. yang, etc.

The Mental Consciousness Structure: configures with the Greeks and the Jews and begins to build a bulwark against the power of mythic images by anathematizing them with rational thinking and logic. Thinking is now triadic: past, present, future; thesis, antithesis, synthesis, etc.

The Integral Consciousness Structure: Gebser's phrase, generally, for the epoch of European and American Modernism that stretches from the rise of aperspectival art, beginning with Manet in the 1860s in Paris and goes down to about the time of World War II.

Martin Heidegger:

Heidegger generally divides history into epochs of Being, in which what it means for an entity "to be" has certain connotations and meanings that are specific to that age. For Heidegger, the history of Being begins with the Greeks, as follows:

Being understood as physis: this is the Pre-Socratic understanding of being, in which entities simply arise autonomously, flash forth their essences and then disappear. Being is immanental and embedded in the process of becoming.

Being as eidos: with Plato being becomes divorced from becoming, since the authenticity of Being resides in the transcendence of the Forms and the Ideas that reside elsewhere, but are above the world of becoming, which is now regarded as fallen and therefore de-privileged.

Being as Logos: in the Christian understanding of Being, Being becomes identified with *a* being, namely, God / Christ, who is the ultimate guarantor of all truth.

Being as Vorhandenheit: from about the time of the Renaissance onward being is understood as pure objectivity. It is a realm of pure subjects beholding purely objective objects which are self-sufficient and have been denuded of all concrete qualities. It is a mathematized sort of understanding of being.

Being as event: Heidegger's own understanding of being as an *Ereignis* event in which poets and artists inaugurate new understandings of being in the form of the creation of new works of art that found epochs.

Peter Sloterdijk:

Building off of Heidegger's designation of the so-called "metaphysical age" that begins with Plato (for *him*, whereas I see its origins already being laid down by Moses and Homer), Sloterdijk in the interview book *Neither Sun Nor Death* draws the epochs as follows:

The Pre-Metaphysical Age: this corresponds to Gebser's magical and mythical consciousness structures, in which being-in-the-world meant being in the body of the Great Mother.

The Metaphysical Age: same as in Heidegger, but for Sloterdijk, being-in-the-world means being in the Father (hence, my thesis, in this book, of the Father's theft of the imaginal vulva).

The Post-Metaphysical Age: in which being-in-the-world means being "thrown" into the world, and in which a real "outside" now appears for the first time (as exemplified by Heidegger's *Being and Time*). For Sloterdijk, being-in-the-world is now tantamount to being thrown into a world that is unprotected by any metaphysical immune systems.

Arnold J. Toynbee:

Toynbee, in his later writings, made a distinction between three different generations of civilization:

First Generation: begins as the result of a response to challenges posed in certain geographic locales by mastering difficult environments. Hence, the Egyptians must drain the swamps of the Delta Valley, and the Mesopotamians must learn to master a resource-poor environment between the Two Rivers.

Second Generation: emerges as the response, not to the challenge of a *physical* environment, but to a *social* environment, namely the crumbling of the higher institutions of the First Generation, which leads to the Hebrews and the Greeks, the Hindus and the Chinese all breaking away from disintegrating social structures and forming new societies in response to them.

Third Generation: Begins with the formation of Islam, the Byzantine Society and currently, the West and Russia.

Franz Borkenau:

An obscure Austrian writer of Marxist extraction who wrote mostly during the 1950s and was brought to my attention by Peter Sloterdijk's discussion of him in his little book *Derrida, an Egyptian*. Borkenau read both Oswald Spengler and Arnold Toynbee and developed a theory of the pulsation of attitudes toward the afterlife that is based upon Toynbee's three different generations of civilization, which his model presupposes.

Death Paranoia: characteristic of tribal societies in which death is never natural but always suspected as the result of magical spells or rival shamans.

Death Transcending Attitude: characteristic of Mesopotamia and Egypt, which corresponds to Toynbee's First Generation of civilization. For these civilizations, the afterlife was simply *what mattered* and preparing oneself for it was the primary concern of this life.

Death Accepting Attitude: begins already with the pharaoh Akhenaten's rejection of the funerary cults and the Underworld in favor exclusively of a world governed by the sun god and light. No darkness allowed. Moses and Homer continue the tradition, in which the Underworld now grows dark and becomes an uninteresting place. The great achievements are happening in *this* world, not the dark and gloomy world of shades encountered by Odysseus in *The Odyssey*.

Death Transcending (Redux): with the rise of Christianity, the attitude of the heavenly world being *more important* than the physical world is retrieved from the first generation of civilization. The soul is now thought of as the most important thing there is, and worldly possessions and knowledge about the world is regarded as irrelevant.

Death Accepting (Redux): with the Renaissance, however, the death accepting attitude of the Greeks and the Jews is revived with the arrival of commercial capitalism, trade, exploration and the creation of new epistemes of discourse about the world.

Death Denying: now characteristic of today's society, in which, for the first time in history, both the soul and the afterlife are regarded *as non-existent*. The world is simply a function of material objects changing forms.

Endnotes

Introduction to the Metaphysical Vulva

1. For Derrida's comment, see the entry for "Phallus" in Dylan Evans, *An Introductory Dictionary of Lacanian Psychoanalysis* (London and New York: Routledge, 1996), 146.

2. Jacques-Alain Miller, ed. Jacques Lacan, *The Psychoses: The Seminar of Jacques Lacan, Book III 1955-56* (London & New York: Routledge, 1993), 215.

3. Jean Gebser, *The Ever-Present Origin* (Ohio University Press, 1985), 44ff.

4. Hesiod, *Theogony, Works and Days, Shield*. Trans. Apostolos N. Athanassakis. (Baltimore and London: Johns Hopkins University Press, 1983), 16.

5. Jean Gebser, ibid., 73ff.

6. Martin Heidegger, *Introduction to Metaphysics* (New Have, Connecticut: Yale University, 2014), 102ff.

7. Gilles Deleuze and Felix Guattari, *A Thousand Plateaus: Capitalism and Schizophrenia* (University of Minnesota Press, 1987), 61-62.

8. The essay, "Letter on Humanism" may be found in Martin Heidegger, *Basic Writings* (New York: Harper Perennial, 2008), 213ff.

9. See the essay "What Are Poets For?" in Martin Heidegger, *Poetry, Language, Thought* (New York: Harper Perennial, 1975), 87ff.

10. See the essay "The Question Concerning Technology" in Martin Heidegger, *The Question Concerning Technology and Other Essays* (New York: Harper Torchbooks, 1977), 3ff.

Opening Title Sequence

11. Jean Gebser, ibid., 261-262.

12. Note that Egyptian hieroglyphics can be read from either left to right, right to left or top to bottom depending on which way the tiny visages of the icons are facing. One always reads *against* whichever way they are facing.

13. See Mircea Eliade, *The Forge and the Crucible: the Origins and Structures of Alchemy* (University of Chicago Press, 1962), 51, where Eliade writes: "Like the metallurgist who transforms embryos (i.e. ores) into metals by accelerating the growth already begun inside the Earth-Mother, the alchemist dreams of prolonging this acceleration and crowning it by the final transmutation of all 'base' metals into the 'noble' metal which is gold."

Awakening

14. Paul Scanlon and Michael Gross, *The Book of Alien* (London: Titan Books, 1993), 31.

15. See Appendix I: On the Sign Regimes in *Alien* for further clarification.

16. See the essay "On Nietzsche" in Gunter Figal, ed. *The Heidegger Reader* (Indiana University Press, 2009), 224ff.

The Crew

17. See Marshall McLuhan and Quentin Fiore, *The Medium is the Massage: An Inventory of Effects* (New York: Bantam Books, 1967), 40-41.

18. The term "uteromorphic" comes from Peter Sloterdijk, *Spheres I: Bubbles* (Los Angeles: Semiotexte, 2011), 279.

19. See the chapter in my book entitled "Being Outside the World: Thoughts on the Space Shuttle Disasters," in John David Ebert, *The Age of Catastrophe: Disaster and Humanity in Modern Times* (Jefferson, North Carolina: McFarland Books, 2012), 61ff.

20. See the interview in which Sloterdijk explains these three different types of world island about halfway down the page: "Talking to Myself About the Poetics of Space" which can be found online at: http://www.harvarddesignmagazine.org/issues/30/talking-to-myself-about-the-poetics-of-space

21. See Heiner Muhlmann, *MSC: Maximal Stress Cooperation, The Driving Force of Cultures* (New York: Springer-Verlag, 2005.

22. See Giorgio Agamben, *Homo Sacer: Sovereign Power and Bare Life* (Stanford University Press, 1998).

***Not*-Earth**

23. The earliest discussion in McLuhan's writings of this contrast between "acoustic space" and "visual space" occurs in the 1956 essay entitled "The Media Fit the Battle of Jericho," and which is included as essay #16 in *Marshall McLuhan Unbound* (Corte Madeira, California: Gingko Press, 2005).

24. For Sloterdijk's discussion of the "sonosphere" see the chapter "The Siren Stage: On the First Sonospheric Alliance" in *Spheres I: Bubbles*, ibid., 477ff.

25. See Gebser, ibid., 53-54 for illustrations of the web-like nature of the magical structure.

26. See John White's excellent discussion of this process in his book *The Birth and Rebirth of Pictorial Space* (Icon Editions, 1972).

27. For "logocentric age" see Jacques Derrida, *Of Grammatology* (Baltimore, Maryland: Johns Hopkins University Press, 1976).

The Landing

28. See the drawing on page 51 of Ian Nathan, *Alien Vault: The Definitive Story of the Making of the Film* (Voyageur Press, 2011).

29. For the image of Garuda picking up an elephant in its talons see J.A.B. van Buitenen, trans. *The Mahabharata Book 1: The Book of the Beginning* (University of Chicago Press, 1973), 81-84.

30. Or see the photograph on page 80 of Ian Nathan, *Alien Vault*, ibid.

31. For Zeus's war against the Titans see Hesiod, *Theogony, Works and Days, Shield*, ibid. 26-31. As Apostolos N. Athanassakis translates the key lines: "And though the Titans' spirit was bold / they were vanquished and then hurled beneath the earth / of the wide paths and bound with wracking chains / as deep down below the earth as high is the sky above it / so deep down into the gloomy Tartaros they were cast."

Excursion

32. For Giger's own account of his frustrations in the

movie studio, see H.R. Giger, *Giger's Alien* (Morpheus International, 1991).

33. Ridley Scott's brother Tony Scott, however, made an excellent film that is precisely about the cult of the dead: the 1983 film *The Hunger*, with Catherine Deneuve and David Bowie (based on a novel by Whitley Strieber).

34. For a discussion of the trial of Orestes as the last stand of matriarchy, see J.J. Bachofen, *Myth, Religion and Mother Right* (Princeton University Press, 1967), 158ff. But especially these lines on page 163, in which Bachofen states: "The antithesis is clear: celestial and Olympian is the right of the father, proclaimed by Zeus…and chthonian, subterranean, is the right of the mother; like its advocates, the Erinyes, it springs from the depths of the earth."

Space Jockey

35. See Adrienne Mayor, *The First Fossil Hunters: Paleontology in Greek and Roman Times* (Princeton University Press, 2000), 284.

36. For Sloterdijk's concept of a "negative gynecology" see the chapter "The Retreat Within the Mother: Groundwork for a Negative Gynecology" in *Spheres I: Bubbles*, ibid., 269ff. For the concept of "nobjects," which he has borrowed from the German theoretician Thomas Macho, see the subsequent chapter "Nobjects and Un-Relationships: On the Revision of Psychoanalytical Stage Theory" in the same book pages 291ff.

Eggs

37. See the interview already cited above, "Talking to

Myself About the Poetics of Space," in which Sloterdijk says: "Women's bodies are apartments!…Now something quite incredible happens in the evolutionary line that leads to mammals: The body of the female members of the species is defined as an ecological niche for her progeny. This leads to a dramatic turn inwards in evolution. What we see is a dual use of the female members of the species, as it were: Henceforth they are no longer only egg-laying systems…but they lay eggs within themselves and make their own body available as an ecological niche for their progeny…The result is a type of event that had not existed in the world before: birth."

Face-Hugger

38. This scene was restored only for the 2003 director's cut of the film.

39. See the chapter entitled "Year Zero: Faciality" on page 167ff. For "deterritorialization" and its counter-concept "reterritorialization" see the entry at the back of the book for "Deterritorialization" on pages 508-510. Both references are to be found in Deleuze and Guattari, *A Thousand Plateaus*, ibid.

40. For Sloterdijk's concept of the *detrait*, see *Spheres I: Bubbles*, ibid., 189.

Chest-Burster

41. For an account of the birth of Athena, see Hesiod, ibid. 35-36. After recounting the birth of Zeus, Hesiod interestingly says that Zeus's wife Hera then parthenogenetically gave birth to the blacksmith god Hephaestus in response. Here, the great goddess attempts to reappropriate the metaphysical vulva that has now been taken over by the high gods of the

metaphysical age pantheon.

Epidermis

42. The reference in Athanassakis's translation of Hesiod, ibid., 25, says: "[Zeus] freed from their wretched bonds his father's brothers / Brontes and Steropes and Arges of the bold spirit / whom Ouranos, their father, had thrown into chains / they did not forget the favors he had done them / and they gave him the thunder and the smoky thunderbolt / and lightning, all of which had lain hidden in the earth."

43. For this image, see *H.R. Giger's Necronomicon* (Zurich, Switzerland: Verlags-Unternehmungen, 1984), 65.

Labyrinth

44. See Jean Gebser's little essay "Cave and Labyrinth" in the online journal *Integrative Explorations: Journal of Culture and Consciousness*, January 1997, Vol. 4, No. 1.

45. For Gebser's discussion of the nature of pre-perspectival space, see *The Ever-Present Origin*, ibid., 9-11.

46. For Heidegger on *Vorhandenheit*, see Martin Heidegger, *Being and Time* (New York: Harper Perennial, 1962), 67-68.

Ash

47. For his comments on the significance of the Amazon rebellions, see J.J. Bachofen, *Myth, Religion and Mother Right*, ibid., 100-109.

48. See John David Ebert, *Rage and the Word: Gilgamesh, Akhenaten, Moses and the Birth of the Metaphysical Age* (Eugene, Oregon: Post-Egoism Media, 2014).

49. See the essay entitled "The Antinomy of Death and the Culture Generations," in Franz Borkenau, *End and Beginning: On the Generations of Cultures and the Origins of the West* (New York: Columbia University Press, 1981).

50. Erwin Rohde, *Psyche: The Cult of Souls and the Belief in Immortality Among the Greeks, Volume 1* (New York: Harper Torchbooks, 1966).

Auto-Destruct

51. Arnold J. Toynbee, *A Study of History, Abridgement of Volumes I-VI* (New York: Oxford University Press, 1987), 255.

52. Jean Baudrillard, *The Transparency of Evil* (London and New York: Verso Books, 1993).

Bibliography

Agamben, Giorgio. *Homo Sacer: Sovereign Power and Bare Life*. Stanford University Press, 1998.

Bachofen, J.J. *Myth, Religion and Mother Right*. Princeton University Press, 1967.

Baudrillard, Jean. *The Transparency of Evil*. London and New York: Verso Books, 1993.

Borkenau, Franz. *End and Beginning: On the Generations of Cultures and the Origins of the West*. New York: Columbia University Press, 1981.

Deleuze, Gilles and Guattari, Felix. *A Thousand Plateaus: Schizophrenia and Capitalism.* University of Minnesota Press, 1987.

Derrida, Jacques. *Of Grammatology*. Baltimore, Maryland: Johns Hopkins University Press, 1976.

Ebert, John David. *The Age of Catastrophe: Disaster and Humanity in Modern Times*. Jefferson, North Carolina: McFarland Books, 2012.

___. *Rage and the Word: Gilgamesh, Akhenaten, Moses and the Birth of the Metaphysical Age*. Eugene, Oregon: Post-Egoism Media, 2014.

Eliade, Mircea. *The Forge and the Crucible: the Origins and Structures of Alchemy*. University of Chicago Press, 1962.

Evans, Dylan. *An Introductory Dictionary of Lacanian Psychoanalysis*. London and New York: Routledge, 1996.

Figal, Gunter, ed. *The Heidegger Reader*. Indiana University Press, 2009.

Gebser, Jean. "Cave and Labyrinth." *Integrative Explorations: Journal of Culture and Consciousness.* January 1997, Vol. 4, No. 1.

___. *The Ever-Present Origin.* Ohio University Press, 1985.

Giger, H.R. *Giger's Alien.* Morpheus International, 1991.

___. *H.R. Giger's Necronomicon.* Zurich, Switzerland: Verlag-Unternehmungen, 1984.

Heidegger, Martin. *Basic Writings.* New York: Harper Perennial, 2008.

___. *Being and Time.* New York: Harper Perennial, 1962.

___. *Introduction to Metaphysics.* New Haven, Connecticut: Yale University, 2014.

___. *Poetry, Language, Thought.* New York: Harper Perennial, 1975.

___. *The Question Concerning Technology and Other Essays.* New York: Harper Torchbooks, 1977.

Hesiod, *Theogony, Works and Days, Shield.* Apostolos N. Athanassakis, trans. Baltimore and London: Johns Hopkins University Press, 1983.

Mayor, Adrienne. *The First Fossil Hunters: Paleontology in Greek and Roman Times.* Princeton University Press, 2000.

McLuhan, Marshall. *Marshall McLuhan Unbound.* Corte Madeira, California: Gingko Press, 2005.

McLuhan, Marshall and Fiore, Quentin. *The Medium is the Massage: An Inventory of Effects.* New York: Bantam Books, 1967.

Miller, Jacques-Alain, ed. Jacques Lacan, *The Psychoses: The Seminar of Jacques Lacan, Book III 1955-56.* London and New York: Routledge, 1993.

Muhlmann, Heiner. *MSC: Maximal Stress Cooperation, The Driving Force of Cultures.* New York: Springer-Verlag, 2005.

Nathan, Ian. *Alien Vault: The Definitive Story of the Making of the Film*. Voyageur Press, 2011.

Rohde, Erwin. *Psyche: The Cult of Souls and the Belief in Immortality Among the Greeks, Volume 1*. New York: Harper Torchbooks, 1966.

Scanlon, Paul and Gross, Michael. *The Book of Alien*. London: Titan Books, 1993.

Sloterdijk, Peter. *Derrida, an Egyptian*. Cambridge, UK: Polity Press, 2009.

___. *Neither Sun Nor Death*. Los Angeles: Semiotexte, 2011.

___. *Spheres I: Bubbles*. Los Angeles: Semiotexte, 2011.

Toynbee, Arnold J. A Study of History, Abridgement of Volumes I-VI. New York: Oxford University Press, 1987.

Van Buitenen, J.A.B., trans. *The Mahabharata Book I: The Book of the Beginning*. University of Chicago Press, 1973.

White, John. *The Birth and Rebirth of Pictorial Space*. Icon Editions, 1972.

Printed in Great Britain
by Amazon